DATE DUE

BRODART, CO.   Cat. No. 23-221

THE
PERFORMANCE
PIPELINE

THE
PERFORMANCE
PIPELINE

GETTING THE RIGHT
PERFORMANCE
AT EVERY LEVEL OF
LEADERSHIP

STEPHEN DROTTER

JOSSEY-BASS
A Wiley Imprint
www.josseybass.com

Published by Jossey-Bass
A Wiley Imprint
989 Market Street, San Francisco, CA 94103-1741—www.josseybass.com

Jossey-Bass books and products are available through most bookstores. To contact
Jossey-Bass directly call our Customer Care Department within the U.S. at 800-956-
7739, outside the U.S. at 317-572-3986, or fax 317-572-4002.

Wiley also publishes its books in a variety of electronic formats and by print-on-demand.
Not all content that is available in standard print versions of this book may appear or be
packaged in all book formats. If you have purchased a version of this book that did not
include media that is referenced by or accompanies a standard print version, you may
request this media by visiting http://booksupport.wiley.com. For more information about
Wiley products, visit us at www.wiley.com.

Library of Congress Cataloging-in-Publication Data
Drotter, Stephen J.
  The performance pipeline : getting the right performance at every level
of leadership / Stephen Drotter.—1st ed.
    p. cm.
  Includes bibliographical references and index.
  ISBN 978-0-470-87728-9 (hardback); ISBN 978-1-118-08646-9 (ebk);
ISBN 978-1-118-08648-3 (ebk); ISBN 978-1-118-08659-9 (ebk)
  1. Leadership. 2. Performance. 3. Management. 4. Organizational
behavior. I. Title.
  HD57.7D76 2011
  658.4'092—dc23
                          2011021312

Printed in the United States of America
FIRST EDITION
HB Printing   10 9 8 7 6 5 4 3 2 1

To Lynn, Stephanie, and Eric
Family is everything!

Contents

Preface

It has become clear to me that leaders everywhere make the same major mistake: they work at the wrong level. In other words, they personally produce results that should be generated at lower levels. This mistake is readily observable in every major industry around the world. What I see most often is leaders spending much of their time solving today's problems personally and not spending enough time anticipating and planning for the future or developing their people. Business performance suffers because leaders are not prepared for the inevitable new challenges. *The Performance Pipeline* addresses this deep-seated, long-standing problem by defining the purpose for each layer of the organization and the specific results required of leaders at that layer to ensure long- and short-term business success. Further, to make people below them successful, leaders have to pass down the things required for them to succeed. These are also spelled out in *The Performance Pipeline*.

This book reveals how work flows from top to bottom and defines the results each layer must produce as well as what each layer must pass down to make the layers below successful. Over the last forty years I have worked with over one hundred companies on five continents for a week or more, assessed over 1,400 leaders, completed over forty CEO succession plans, and conducted several hundred work interviews (designed to learn what leaders actually do). This book is based on what I have observed, learned, and practiced. Its premise, borne out by my experience, is that leaders develop best when they pursue the results that are right for their layer. This in turn makes businesses more likely to succeed. Contrary to other schools of thought, I have discovered that focusing on behavior has some value but does not produce the needed development because the new behavior is too often applied to the wrong work.

Ten years ago, a book called *The Leadership Pipeline*, which I coauthored, was published. New language and a new framework were introduced that changed the dialogue on leadership development and succession planning. *The Leadership Pipeline* is now known and accepted worldwide. One critical Leadership Pipeline idea that has added particular value is that transitions from one layer of the organization to the next are major events requiring changes in skills, work values, and time horizons. I have been asked repeatedly by leaders at every level for help on making these transitions. In *The Performance Pipeline* I address these transition challenges on the basis of ten years of new learnings and practices for transition management. Knowing the specific results required at each layer helps everyone understand more precisely what these transitions mean to the business and to the leader.

The Performance Pipeline addresses three critical business needs:

1. How to improve business performance by defining the unique purpose of each organization layer and providing clarity and focus on the results to be achieved. That is what a performance pipeline does.

2. How to make all leaders successful by having leaders at every layer pass down to the layers below them the things that leaders there need in order to be successful.

3. How to help leaders make the transition to a new layer and how to remove performance roadblocks so that leaders can deliver the results required at their new layer.

My overarching goal for this book is to help leaders get the results they need in today's highly uncertain business environment.

Seeing the work of leaders as *results* to be achieved expressed as performance standards in the areas of finance/operations, leadership, management, relationships, and innovation, rather than as a set of *behaviors*, is the key. Addressing the problem of the leader working at the wrong layer, which I described earlier as universal, is also a major objective.

Given the increasing importance, and difficulty, of achieving desired results for all businesses, I hope you will find this book both timely and useful.

July 2011

Stephen Drotter
Carlsbad, California

Part I

The Performance Pipeline Concept

Introduction

Dealing with Pervasive Uncertainty

While a Performance Pipeline would have helped organizations years ago, current events and trends make it even more useful today. Let's start out by examining how an uncertain and rapidly changing environment drives organizations toward the Performance Pipeline model.

We have entered a period of great confusion and volatility for business and its leaders. Executives at all levels have to deliver results under difficult and changing conditions. We are uncertain about a wide variety of issues, including

- The rate and nature of the recovery from the Global Financial Crisis

- Economic viability of customers and key suppliers

- The shifting balance of economic power

- Changes in consumer spending

- When and how to invest capital

- Finding needed skills in the available labor pool

- The consequence of government decisions on tax rates and regulation

- Commodity and scarce resource prices

Combined, these and other external uncertainties put leaders at every level under great stress and every business in a high-risk situation.

At the same time, businesses are living with great internal uncertainties—about organization capability, leadership effectiveness, alignment of priorities, ability to get all the work done, legal compliance, and the like. While these uncertainties have always existed, they are less tolerable in a more economically challenging environment. We can no longer accept leaders who don't work on defining and delivering the future, who don't work collaboratively with the rest of the organization, who don't know what their people are doing, who don't develop their people, and who don't learn themselves. In a highly uncertain external environment, we should be making every effort to build more certainty in our internal environment—in the organization's ability to perform. In the same way a violinist must know what her instrument will do when played faster or slower and with more pressure or less, we need to know what our organizations will do when strategy must change, when operating conditions change, or when customers' needs change. We need to know that our leaders can handle the new challenges. Without a performance architecture that defines exactly what every leader at every level must produce for the business, all this change and uncertainty will blindside companies. That's one reason the Performance Pipeline is such a timely tool.

Dramatic Changes in the World Economy Make Matters Worse

During boom years, there is room for error and inefficiency. Businesses make money and grow despite their shortcomings. Fueled by growth in India, China, and other developing nations as well as insatiable consumer demand that powered unprecedented consumer spending in the developed world, the global economy boomed. Winners were everywhere, and internal structural problems were papered over with profitable growth. Then, abruptly, it was over; the economy crashed. The Global Financial Crisis affected every business. Downsizing, outsourcing, and in some cases disappearance became the orders of the day for businesses around the world. Dramatic action was required, and painful choices were made. Survival was, and still is at this writing, a fundamental driver of leadership effort.

As we slowly climb out of the recession, we face many critical questions and the uncertainty seems even greater. How fast will the recovery happen? How should our strategy change in light of the uncertainty? How quickly should we rebuild inventory? When should we begin to hire, and how many people should we bring in? Where can we get the capital we need for investment; where should we invest and how quickly? What changes are likely in health care and in taxes, and how do we respond?

As a direct consequence of the uncertainty exemplified by these questions, every leader's job has gotten harder. Under this kind of pressure, leaders at all levels have become focused on the short term and reactive just when they need to be looking forward and planning rigorously.

As leaders attempt to address these externally driven challenges, they will need new solutions and much more alignment and flexibility inside their companies to be sure they can respond effectively. Going back to old practices developed to address a very different set of business conditions doesn't make any sense. Leaders at every level need to think more broadly, find new methods, provide greater clarity, and enable sharper focus. These must become the guiding ideas for leaders at all levels. Delivering the right results at the right time in the right way has to be primary, and new tools and practices are required to do it. We must make a fundamental shift in our basic leadership practices if we are to succeed in this uncertain environment. As we'll see, the Pipeline model makes this shift possible.

Four Imperatives

I would like to focus your attention on four key imperatives for leaders in our current environment. These imperatives dovetail with the changes sweeping through organizations today; the Performance Pipeline makes it possible to address these imperatives. Before looking at how the Pipeline does so, let's look at the four imperatives and why they must be addressed.

1. Thinking More, Learning More

Thinking about the current performance and future direction of your business or function has to include major economic trends, world political events, currency fluctuations, new competitors, global best practice, rapidly evolving technology that is changing how we work, consumer preferences in many countries, and so on. Specific needs associated with your products, customers, suppliers, competitors, likely new market entrants, and your workforce change *how* you look at the world, not *whether* you should look at it. We all have to consider a wider range of variables. Learning about the world around us requires time every day.

Fortunately we have computers and the Internet to help with information flow and retrieval. Although we cannot trust it implicitly, information is plentiful in cyberspace. Before we make decisions, however, this information must be validated by firsthand experience, personal observations, and input from trusted sources. We also have to think carefully about what the information means once we are satisfied it is valid, since the context in which we work has changed.

Thinking takes time. The more variables we must consider, the more time we need to think. As you no doubt are aware, leaders lack thinking time. Meetings from morning to night, one hundred or more e-mails per day, voice mail, family demands, and travel are the norm. Thinking deeply and reflectively under these conditions is difficult. We become caught in "activity traps" and thus fail to think and learn.

THE FIRST IMPERATIVE: *Every leader spends thirty minutes to one hour or more daily in uninterrupted thought.*

2. New Methods for Almost Everything

It isn't an exaggeration to say that most businesses need new methods for just about everything they do—a rapidly changing environment demands it. Unfortunately, most companies are better at squelching new ideas than they are at encouraging them. Think about what happened to the last new idea you put forward. How long ago was it? How was it received? What was the result? How do you feel about putting forward another new idea?

In the midst of all the chaos that exists in most companies, new ideas often aren't heard. Loud, powerful voices defend the status quo at strategy and budget meetings. There isn't enough time for creative thinking, and even if there is, the culture or management may eschew the risk that comes with "new." So, we do the same old things but perhaps a little cheaper or a little faster. It is so much easier to just keep doing what we did yesterday.

THE SECOND IMPERATIVE: *Everyone must innovate as a natural and expected part of one's daily routine.*

3. Clarity of Role and Purpose

When people show up for work, they should know what is expected of them, when it is due, what the cost should be, and what standards must be met. Everyone wants to know these things. Management practices commonly used now don't deliver role clarity. In fact, many current practices confuse rather than clarify.

While balanced scorecards are valuable frameworks for directing and measuring team or business performance, they don't tell individuals what they should work on and are usually silent on leadership work. Strategy is critically important for the business but generally doesn't naturally penetrate to lower levels. Strategy needs to be translated downward, layer by layer, but seldom is. Lower layers are left with the responsibility for interpreting what their contributions should be. Several recent studies on this subject concluded that employees at the bottom are more likely to do what they have been doing even if it doesn't fit the strategy. Goals and key performance indicators (KPIs) tend to be operationally focused or financially oriented. They are great as far as they go, but softer parts of leadership work don't often make the list.

Company programs for developing leaders are designed generically and focus on corporate citizenship. They don't help much with clarifying the role and purpose of an individual job. How to do your specific job is rarely taught.

THE THIRD IMPERATIVE: *Leaders must provide true role clarity and purpose for every employee.*

4. A Focus on Delivering Value

Leaders who are tied up all day in meetings, who spend their time "doing," and who work at the layer they came from, or even lower, rather than at the layer to which they are assigned, don't add enough value. They can't possibly engage properly with their people. As a consequence the priorities are often unclear or nonexistent for their teams. The proper focus required to deliver the right results at the right time in the right way is missing. Extraneous or simply urgent matters override important work. Well-meaning and motivated employees do what they think is right, but it often is disconnected from what really adds value.

Electronic traffic—e-mail, voice mail, instant messages, and the like—provides speed of communication. It also destroys concentration and focus. Our lives, both at work and at home, are overrun by these electronic intrusions. It seems that any electronic message or phone call is more important than what is going on face to face or what you are doing by yourself. It has never been harder to focus for an extended period than it is right now. It also seems that communication between leaders and their people has never been worse.

Some highly regarded management tools and Human Resource programs actually cause focus to be on activity rather than results. Competency models are widely used and accepted. In their original form they were meant to spell out how specific job families were to achieve specific results under specific circumstances. Now they are generally applied to all job families and are completely disconnected from results under specific circumstances.

THE FOURTH IMPERATIVE: *Leaders must create an environment where sufficient focus is achievable.*

The Performance Pipeline Concept

To respond to these four imperatives, you don't need an expensive "change management" program or a new CEO. Rather, a top-to-bottom architecture that distributes the accountability by layer and defines how work flows down to the appropriate layer is what's needed. This architecture, the Performance Pipeline, was developed to help leaders increase think time, encourage innovation, provide clarity, and enable focus.

The Performance Pipeline architecture is based on these ideas:

- Every layer has a unique purpose.

- Every layer delivers unique results.

- Every layer contributes to the success of the layers below.

- All layers are connected, not gapped or overlapped.

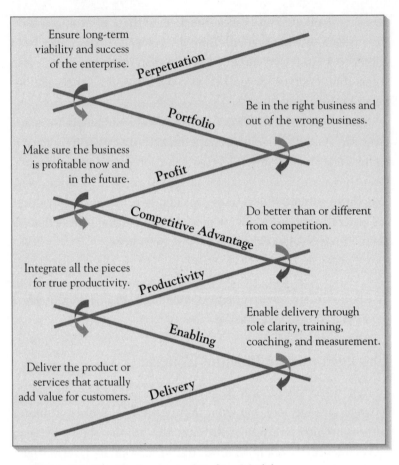

Ensure long-term
viability and success
of the enterprise.   Perpetuation

Portfolio   Be in the right business and
out of the wrong business.

Make sure the business
is profitable now and
in the future.   Profit

Competitive Advantage   Do better than or different
from competition.

Integrate all the pieces
for true productivity.   Productivity

Enabling   Enable delivery through
role clarity, training,
coaching, and measurement.

Deliver the product or
services that actually
add value for customers.   Delivery

Figure I.1 The Performance Pipeline Model

Translated into visual form, the Performance Pipeline model for a big company looks like Figure I.1.

Now let's examine each "turn" in the Performance Pipeline. I realize that some of the following may seem obvious; bear in mind that the value of the Pipeline is how it focuses attention on each layer's results, and on the interconnectedness of the layers. The Pipeline provides a total picture for making the whole enterprise efficient and effective. After the following brief descriptions of each layer, we'll be better able to discuss the Pipeline's value to organizations and to see how it operates.

The person at the very top is responsible for defining what the enterprise should look like in the long-term future. She collects information from large groups of customers, external partners, associates, and governments. She makes decisions about future requirements based on a forecast of future conditions in the world, the market, and the industry. She also decides what the internal architecture must be. These decisions are expressed as a *corporate strategic framework*. Definitions of vision, mission, and values are often included.

The layer just below uses the corporate strategic framework as the basis for evaluating the longer-term fit and viability of current business and likely areas of exploration for new business. A *portfolio strategy* is defined, enabled by an investment plan and a succession plan.

The next layer down produces a *business strategy* and delivers short- and long-term profit based on its position in the portfolio and the capital made available to it. This layer assembles a multi-functional team and gets the team to work together.

Using the business strategy for guidance, the layer below determines how to achieve a competitive advantage for the business through the effort of the function they run. Appropriate *functional capability*—people, methods, and partnerships—is acquired and installed.

The next layer uses the functional capability to deliver productivity, trained management, and information flow, holding everyone to the standards and ensuring delivery of the competitive advantage. An *operating plan* captures the actions to be taken.

Within the context of the operating plan, the layer below delivers *clearly defined roles, trained people, feedback, and coaching* to enable delivery.

At the bottom level, individual contributors produce the designs, products, sales, distribution, and the services and support for all of these according to the timetable and standards set by their leader.

Now with these foundational elements in mind, consider if your organization connects the dots from layer to layer. In other words, does it translate strategy into roles and responsibilities unique to each layer, and does it attempt to coordinate the work and results produced so that overlaps and gaps between layers are minimized?

How the Leadership Pipeline Produced the Performance Pipeline

The Leadership Pipeline model (Figure I.2) has been used in many companies, including Johnson & Johnson, Marriott, IBM, Microsoft, Gap, Newmont Mining, and Citigroup, in the United States; British American Tobacco, Aker Solutions, and Coca-Cola Hellenic, in Europe; Westpac, BHP, and QR National, in Australia; and De Beers, Sasol, and Murray & Roberts, in South Africa. The Leadership Pipeline presents a model for looking at leadership work and career development. At each passage, important changes are required in skills, time application, and work values because the required results change and the time horizon extends further into the future.

My work with these organizations and many, many more not only helped clarify my thinking about the Leadership Pipeline, but it demonstrated the need for companion architecture to help each company define required results for each layer and provide a basis for transition from concept to useful tool. Defining required results by layer gives additional meaning and utility to the Leadership Pipeline. Career guidance, planning for development, succession planning, and course work all gain deeper meaning when the required results are identified. The two concepts work hand in hand. By defining the required results and downward flow of requirements (the Performance Pipeline) and the upward flow of leadership careers (the Leadership Pipeline), organizations can ground their performance and development in their critical business needs.

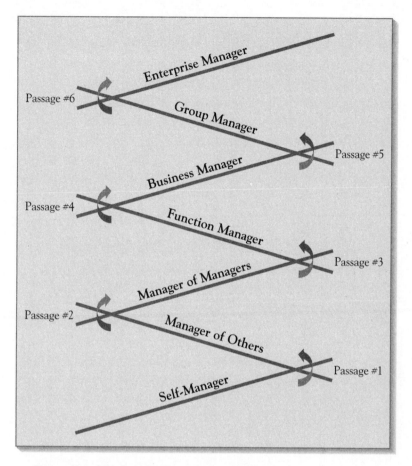

Figure I.2 The Leadership Pipeline Model

In Table I.1 the two Pipelines are combined. From this point on, I'm going to be using Leadership Pipeline terminology for each layer—just glance at Figure I.2 and Table I.1, and you'll quickly become familiar with the key terms.

Business Case for the Performance Pipeline

Whenever it comes to a new model, the question is always whether implementation is worth it. There is always a learning curve to climb. There are always naysayers to convince. In my implementation

Table 1.1 The Leadership Pipeline with the Performance Pipeline

Leadership Pipeline: Passage	Performance Pipeline: Business Purpose/Contribution	Focus
Enterprise Manager	Perpetuate the enterprise/ Enterprise strategic framework	What should this enterprise look like in twenty to fifty years? How will we get the resources we need?
Group Manager	Right portfolio/Portfolio strategy; strategic differentiation for business investment; business general manager succession	Do we have the right collection of businesses? What should be added or removed? Are we developing people to run our businesses both today and tomorrow?
Business Manager	Profit, long- and short-term/ Strategy, including products, markets, customers, etc.	Do our products/services add appropriate value for our customers, shareholders, and employees? How should our strategy change if we want to fit the portfolio and add more value?
Function Manager	Competitive advantage/Functional excellence	How can we do this better than our competitors? Do we have the right functional capability?
Manager of Managers	Productivity/Integration and focus; capable managers	Do I have the right leaders and the best processes? Are they working together?
Manager of Others	Enable delivery/Assignment clarity and coaching	Are my people trained and motivated to add value for customers? Do I have the right mix of talent?
Self-Manager (Individual Contributor)	Delivery/Customer satisfaction	Am I doing my best to deliver the right product/service? Am I being a good corporate citizen?

of Performance Pipeline concepts in organizations throughout the world, I've found that using the Pipeline approach is more than worth it. The benefits aren't simply incremental or limited to one area. From what I've observed and what I've heard later from leaders of these companies, the benefits of using results with performance standards differentiated by layer include these:

1. Clear differentiation of the results required, by layer, enables *better results through improved clarity and focus for all leaders.* Everyone is able to understand the work required by his layer. While good organization design is supposed to accomplish this, most design effort is spent on the horizontal structure. My work with organizations has convinced me that the bulk of the problems exist in the vertical structure. Identifying specific purposes for each layer helps cut through the clutter of daily work life that exists in the vertical structure.

2. *The demand for leaders can be reduced.* Operating with fewer but better leaders is now possible because spans of control can be greater if all the leaders understand their purpose, work at the right level, and stop doing the work from their previous level.

3. Measuring all the required results, not just the financial results, enables better performance and *drives development from the work itself.* Both objective and subjective measures are needed, and both kinds work.

4. Clear definition by layer enables *transparency.* A chief executive sitting in Athens, Greece, can have a clear picture of the work being done by a first-line manager in Moscow, Russia. A few simple questions can validate that understanding or signal a problem to be addressed.

5. *Decision making about people improves* dramatically. Selection decisions in particular are improved by enabling better specifications for the position and better performance data on

the candidates. By using a more complete set of measures, it is easier to tell who should move up and who shouldn't. Consistent standards for these decisions improve consistency across the enterprise.

6. *Leadership time is spent more appropriately* because all leaders know the results they must deliver in order to work at the right level. Well-paid senior leaders are measured on doing more sophisticated work. The vast majority of product and service work is done by the lower level and lower-paid people. The problem of paying executive prices for "getting the windows washed" goes away. Also, the scope of all leadership positions is expanded at no extra cost.

7. *Development and coaching have clear, results-based targets,* producing better business outcomes for the time and money invested. Coaching becomes purpose-driven, and development outcomes become measurable.

Other benefits besides these seven exist, including alignment of all Human Resource programs and consistency of performance measurement across functions and businesses. Rather than detail all the benefits, I would simply ask that you keep the following overarching benefit in mind: the Performance Pipeline changes the source code on the human side of the business. *It shifts the focus from behavioral science or activity to results differentiated by layer.* In short, leadership and management are defined as results.

Leadership Development Frustrations . . . and Solutions

Companies have benefited from the Performance Pipeline in many ways, and I'm going to share their stories throughout the book. Here, though, I want to zoom in on one particularly significant way that the Performance Pipeline helps organizations: leadership development. This is such a critical issue when it comes to building sustainable enterprises, and it's also one that causes many management groups sleepless nights and stress-filled days.

Ask yourself why your organization doesn't have enough good leaders. You are hiring "A players." You have a wide range of leadership development programs. Everyone loves your competency model. Coaches are all over your business or company. Succession planning is done religiously.

Every year, I receive many calls about this issue. The callers insist that they are doing everything right, yet their leadership development is all wrong. Here are three typical calls and capsule descriptions of how the Pipeline model revealed what needed to be changed:

Case 1

"We are having trouble developing Country Business Managers even though we have a broad range of leadership development programs. We have to go outside for talent way too often."

What I found was an excessive focus on sales and revenue, and not enough emphasis on getting results in strategy and planning, people development, and organization-building at all levels. Jobs were defined too simplistically. Country Business Managers and their direct reports were measured and focused like salesmen.

Case 2

"We have a broad array of leadership development programs; we run them all over the world. One magazine gave us an award for being the best. We have a large staff of management development experts, but there isn't any cumulative effect. We don't have five years' worth of progress from five years' worth of effort."

What I found was undifferentiated attendance at programs; that is, employees from several different levels attended the courses at the same time. These courses encouraged leaders at different layers to do the same things, not different things. Also, the course content changed as the person in charge of the course work changed. Without a performance anchor, each new leadership development leader changed content according to his view of requirements.

Case 3

"We have formed a task force to figure out how to address the upcoming mass exodus of leaders. We do succession planning, we run many leadership development programs, and we have external coaches here every day, yet we don't have any bench strength."

What I found was that the key layer for addressing their bench strength issues—the Managers of Managers—was not being asked to develop or manage to a budget. These managers were not asked to participate in strategy development. They were not held accountable for developing successors. Consequently, they looked "too narrow" to move up.

These three companies have been very successful for a long time. You would be proud to work for any of them. Great people work there, and the companies invest heavily in leadership development. Yet they were all committing a leadership development sin. All of them had chosen the wrong starting point. People and programs are not what leadership development should be about. Getting the work done is what matters. These companies failed to define the work *appropriately*, so the number one leadership development tool—the work itself—was hindering the development of the incumbents. Courses and coaches don't fix this problem.

From working with these and other clients, I drew two conclusions:

1. Successful leadership development starts with defining completely the results to be achieved.
2. The Leadership Pipeline is of more value if you are clear about the results to be achieved.

Establishing the work to be done at each layer and creating standards for measuring performance must be done before the Leadership Pipeline can be used effectively. This is where the Performance Pipeline comes in. It is the starting point for leadership development, and it enables delivering the right results in the right way at the right time.

What You Will Read

The central idea of *The Performance Pipeline* is that a unique purpose and measurable results can and should be established for each layer of the organization. In Part II, in defining the results to be expected from each layer, I focus first on the most critical results relative to the layer's unique purpose. Expected results may include some important but overlooked or misunderstood results that make a difference. There may also be some results that underpin better-known results. For example, competitive analysis underpins strategy. Those results will be summarized and listed, along with the enabling results that must be passed down to the next level. An actual, in-use definition of the total set of results and the expected performance standards will also be presented. These whole pictures were developed at successful enterprises and are being used now. The names of enterprises will be withheld in order to protect their privacy. To help diagnose any problems, I have identified results that are commonly but erroneously delivered by each layer.

Making the layers below successful is another central idea of *The Performance Pipeline*. Each layer must contribute a few key results that help those below understand what to do and how to do it.

The chapters in Part III address the most important implementation challenges. Removing the inevitable, deep-seated performance roadblocks that exist in most companies is discussed at length. A new method for enabling the transition from one layer to the next is spelled out in some detail. Other actions required for success, based on actual experience, are in the concluding chapter.

As you read this book, I hope you will see how to embrace uncertainty rather than fear it, how to seek new experiences rather than avoid them, and how to broaden leadership capability, not narrow it, as you face your daily challenges in a highly uncertain business environment.

You may find it helpful to look at an actual performance pipeline before reading further. In the back of the book, Tool 1 is a complete performance pipeline in use today. This book will tell you how to build one yourself, and use it.

1

Defining Your Performance Pipeline

The Global Financial Crisis of 2008–2009 has provided compelling evidence for why organizations need a performance pipeline—as well as evidence that many companies lacked such a pipeline during this massive economic downturn. Consider the following questions and whether you could have answered them then—and now:

- Do you know what every leader in your organization is trying to achieve today; do you have a convenient way to find out?

- Are all critical results assigned?

- Are requirements for full performance clear to every leader?

- Is every leader working at the level to which he or she is assigned?

- Is the right work being done in the right way?

- Do you know which leaders are inhibiting the performance of the people who report to them?

- Are you clear about your own role?

Over the last several years and especially during the financial tumult, I found that many leaders couldn't answer these questions. It seemed that no one knew what was really getting done. While companies may be able to avoid these questions during periods of growth and economic stability, they can't ignore them during any type of crisis or any significant period of change. As observed in the Introduction, we live in extremely volatile times; even if companies emerging from the Global Financial Crisis are doing well, they are likely to face many other challenges around the corner. If they are not able to answer these questions, they will struggle with this challenge.

Facilitating answering these questions for leaders has been my mission in recent years, and it has motivated me to define the Performance Pipeline.

Reflect on your answers to these questions. If your answer to any of them is no, you need a performance pipeline to help you get to a yes. Goals and KPIs (key performance indicators) aren't enough, because they don't encompass all leadership, management, or relationship results. The budget and the strategy aren't reliable indicators of what is being done today—in fact, they are usually misinterpreted or not guiding the work for other reasons. When this is realized, it provides a strong incentive to implement the Pipeline process.

Yet how do you implement it? At first blush, the need to define all results at each leadership level may feel like an overwhelming task. Let me assure you, it's eminently doable, as long as you follow a tested process and benefit from the experiences of those who have gone before you.

The Performance Pipeline process consists of the following six steps:

- Defining the purpose—being clear about what outcome you want
- Collecting the data—finding out what's really getting done, or not getting done but should be
- Sorting and codifying the data—organizing data in a useful way
- Defining the results to be delivered at each layer and the standards for measuring those results

- Validating the standards—getting leaders to agree

- Allowing some flexibility—allowing different groups to adapt the standards in order to reflect specific needs

I'll next discuss each of these six process steps in detail, referring also to examples in Tool 1 at the end of the book, which should make it easier to understand and use the information provided. And I'll include boxes, "Lessons Learned," which will share the knowledge that comes from hard experience—my own as well as the hundred or so companies that have used this Pipeline process. In fact, let's begin with the first and one of the most important lessons.

Lessons Learned
Most leadership performance problems can be traced to the vertical structure

The questions at the beginning of this chapter relate to organization, and organization is the *black hole* of business. Great effort (energy in) seems to produce little improvement (nothing out). Almost all of the effort goes into the horizontal structure—deciding whether to organize around customers or functions or geography or products or business units is the great debate. There are only a few choices for the horizontal structure. While the horizontal structure is important, the vertical structure is where the real problems reside. Gaps between layers due to managers not managing, overlaps resulting from micromanagement, doing lower-level work at higher layers, and defining lower-level jobs too narrowly create performance problems at many companies. These vertical problems are close to infinite in number and deserve much more attention. Not only do they hinder performance; they also block transparency and hurt leadership development.

As you may have suspected by this point, thinking of the Performance Pipeline as an organization model for distributing work is appropriate. It distributes work from top to bottom, from strategy to low-level tasks. To get full value, you should develop your company's own unique version and not just use a generic version or copy one from another company. The process for developing your company's unique model is actually quite simple. A small team of people can complete it in about ten work days if they have a basic knowledge of the company, the business, and the work being done, as well as some experience in structured interviewing techniques.

You don't have to reinvent the wheel. If you want to design a performance pipeline to fit your organization, you can benefit from the methodology I've used in the last twenty years of practice. The essence of this methodology are the six process steps just bulleted. Let's look at each of these steps in detail, thinking about the lessons learned regarding these steps and how you can apply these lessons in your design.

Defining the Purpose

Companies that have made the most progress in creating and using performance pipelines were clear at the outset about why they were doing it. So before you do anything else, decide what business outcomes or benefits you want the model to deliver. It will help in choosing the right work and setting appropriate standards. From companies I've worked with, here are some examples of their purpose in creating a performance pipeline:

- Moving more authority and ownership for results to lower levels (mining)

- Improving the development of Country Business Managers (fast-moving consumer goods)

- Enabling expansion to new geographies or countries (software, lodging)

- Changing the focus and clarifying the expected contribution of all leaders (transportation)

- Transforming the company (consumer goods)

- Improving leadership development (construction, financial services)

- Facilitating cost reduction (pharmaceuticals)

Other purposes are fine. The key is that you're clear about your purpose when you reach the validation phase. And since many people will be interviewed during the data collection phase, they will need to hear why you are doing it.

Before you begin, spend time thinking about and discussing what you would like to change or improve about how your business operates, and/or the work of your leaders, in order to improve your business results or your company's success. Consider what is and isn't getting done at each leadership layer separately and collectively. Your performance pipeline can be used to assign work that isn't getting done, provide emphasis to an area needing improvement, move work done to lower layers, and provide more challenge in the day-to-day work to help leaders develop.

For your organization to function at a high level, the layers have to be connected, not gapped and not overlapped. Changes at one layer will affect the layers immediately above and below because of supervisory requirements above and response requirements below. Changes in accountability ripple up and down, so if you change one layer it affects all the other layers. Don't limit your thinking to only one layer. With a well-defined purpose, you will naturally plan with multiple layers in mind; you can link each specific layer to the overall purpose and minimize gaps and overlaps.

Example

I was asked to help a fast-moving consumer goods company develop more effective Business General Managers. They were thinking about this layer in isolation. After conducting work interviews with several Business General Managers, it was clear that they were not developing because they were not asked to do a broad enough job. They were being measured on a very narrow set of results—revenue and volume. When we broadened the range of results to include people development, strategy development and execution, and process improvement, then the measurements and capabilities for their bosses—Group Managers—had to be changed as well to push work down to appropriate levels. Further, the Function Manager positions had to be expanded in order to improve preparation for Business General Manager roles and to accept the functional work that the Business General Managers were currently doing. So some work done by Function Managers had to be pushed down to Managers of Managers to balance the load. Pursuit of improvement at one layer soon turned into changes at every layer.

Because this company had a narrow focus at the outset, they weren't prepared for the cost and time required for the needed solution. Almost a full year was wasted as we worked our way down the organization one layer at a time. When establishing your purpose, it is critical to look at the whole system and not underestimate the amount of change needed at every layer.

Collecting Data

Considerable discipline is required when collecting data because it is the aggregate of all responses that counts, not just one layer's or one person's response. It is common to value a few people or a particular function more than others, but you need the full picture to get the best answer. Interviewers must use a standardized set of questions and be disciplined enough to ask everyone the same questions in the same way.

The other requirement for interviewers is a deep understanding of what constitutes appropriate answers. A standard set of questions will elicit useful responses, but interviewers must interpret those responses and make judgments about how complete and appropriate they are. Follow-up probes are always needed to get the full answer.

Interview Questions

Deciding on the questions to be asked is directly connected to your purpose and to good practice. A core set of questions is required in all performance pipeline building efforts as well as discretionary questions associated with the purpose. Core questions usually

---

Lessons Learned

Leaders are not always fluent in the language of results

A significant number of leaders don't know what results are beyond the financials or their budget. When asked about required results, they list tasks. When asked about tasks required to achieve results, they list activities or say they have already answered. Softer items on the human side of business are viewed as skills needed for activities, not as results. For example, many executives view building an effective team as a skills-based activity rather than as a measurable result—they don't naturally talk about how teams are needed to achieve specific results, so interviewers need to draw this out of them. Profit is an outcome achieved through many underlying results, including a great plan and an effective team. Interviewers must frame their questions with results in mind.

---

address the job itself. Discretionary questions usually cover things like preparation needed, likely changes, unique relationships, and any specific problem or opportunity that interests you.

A set of questions that I commonly use is contained in Tool 2 at the end of this book. The first question, for instance, asks interviewees about the scope of their job. This question helps you understand how a person thinks about the breadth and depth of what he is supposed to contribute. It gives you great insight on how clear he is about his role, how broadly or narrowly he views accountability, and where he thinks he fits in the workings of the business or enterprise. The second question asks about expected results. The subject's answer reveals her mind-set and perspective on results in addition to the actual results as she sees them.

These questions are designed to give you two different sets of information. One is the factual response; the other is mind-set and perspective. You need both sets of information to plan the most useful path forward; changing required results without changing mind-set and perspective won't work. For example, a Function Manager in charge of Sales and Distribution might say, "The results I am expected to deliver are to

- Meet my revenue target

- Be at or below my cost budget

- Hold head count at last year's ending level

- Have 98 percent of all orders shipped on time."

While these factual responses are important, this respondent also demonstrates an execution mind-set. Outcomes associated with business building are not mentioned; this person doesn't address such issues as new customers, people development, teamwork between sales and distribution, or process improvements.

While this individual may pursue some of these business-building items, they won't be measured and accounted for.

Interviewing

Ideally, every leader should be interviewed. Practically, a representative sample at each layer is sufficient. Full participation at the upper layers—Business General Managers, Group Managers, and Enterprise Managers—is crucial for promoting better understanding and acceptance of the end product. For Function Managers, Managers of Managers, and Managers of Others (first-line managers), the representative sample approach is fine. Actual numbers depend on the size of your company or business, but five to ten people per layer are usually enough.

Choose the interviewees carefully. High-performers generally give the best picture of what respondents are doing and why they are doing it; experts tend to provide the greatest insight on what needs to be done to produce great results. In some cases, people new to their jobs or new to the company can offer fresh insight, but most of the time they don't have enough context to be as helpful as you need them to be. Underperformers don't make good subjects.

Make a list of your best performers by layer, and include all the executives. Schedule ninety minutes for each interview; interviews can be completed in sixty minutes, but I have found that people really like to talk about their jobs. In fact, you will probably be the first person they have met in a long time who actually wants to hear about what they do and how they do it. By allowing the interview to "run long," you gain rich answers—information that delves deep into what helps them deliver great results (and sometimes what prevents them from doing so).

At this point, the biggest challenge is making interviewees comfortable. They will want to know what will happen with their answers. Tell them that they are not being judged or assessed, that it's all about the nature of their work, and that answers will be aggregated so that no attribution will be made. All that will be disclosed is their participation.

An opening preamble is also a good idea. A major retailer used this introduction:

> Our goal is to improve overall performance by having the right people in the right job at the right time to take advantage of our growth opportunities.
>
> We are trying to develop a more valid and accurate picture of the work that is done by leaders like you so we can better integrate development into our culture by building useful development, assessment, selection, and coaching tools.
>
> We need your input and that of several other people at all layers. We are after as accurate a description of your work as possible.
>
> You were chosen because it was felt you would do a good job of describing your work and some of the challenges you face. Your answers will be anonymous; all answers will be aggregated by organization layer.
>
> A standardized interview is being used in order to drive consistency. I will read the questions to be sure that everyone is asking the same questions in the same way. Please feel free to ask for clarification or explanation if necessary.

Obviously, you should adapt this preamble to your own particular purpose and situation, though starting out with some version of the first paragraph is a good idea.

Sorting and Codifying the Data

In Aggregate

Ask yourself if the story hangs together. In other words, what conclusions can you draw after reviewing all the answers? Does the

Lessons Learned

The true character of a job is determined by the decisions the incumbent can make and by the obstacles to be overcome

Other factors may impact job character, but these two define the context where the real work sits. Responsibility for decision making defines what you "own." One example: you can describe your job as "responsible for strategy," but if you aren't the one who decides what the final strategy is then you are the strategy analyst or recommender or researcher, not the true strategist. The true strategists make the decision and live with its consequences, so their decision making is much harder. Your recommendations are important, but you aren't really determining the future direction of the company. A second example: when a company with a strong brand and well-developed distribution systems launches a new product, the obstacles differ from those facing a small, unknown company with limited distribution as it launches a new product. Those situations represent two totally different jobs. One job can rely on existing support that has a track record. The other has to overcome major obstacles without existing support. Support will have to be built or bought. Listen carefully to the answers to questions 3A, 3B, and 4 (see Tool 2). Look carefully at the connection between the results to be delivered and the decisions that can be made. Also listen carefully for the presence or absence of support and for established methods versus things that have to be built.

---

amount of time your leaders spend calling on customers suggest that leading and managing the team are taking a backseat? Does the decision-making authority seem reasonable for the expected results they described? Are the obstacles severe or just normal market conditions? The key is looking at the big picture based on all the responses rather than focusing narrowly on a piece of information.

Analysis of the story in total is valuable for making decisions about what standards to choose and how challenging they need to be at each layer.

Looking at the actual work being done and people's understanding of their job, hearing what is "top-of-mind" and what has to be probed for, provides a useful picture of how your leaders really work. In some instances, your aggregated interview data may be sufficiently surprising and compelling that it causes you to reassess your purpose for building a performance pipeline.

Example—Finding Surprises

A major consumer goods company with a large global presence launched an important culture change effort. After completing some very large acquisitions, it wanted to create a new culture that included a uniform work style and a common value system. Strategically, the emphasis was on an aggressive growth objective via finding new products and markets as well as improving the supply chain. The leadership development group needed to create new programs in order to support the culture change. A sampling of fifty leaders from around the world was asked to participate in the work interviews. Seven to ten leaders per layer were interviewed by a small HR team. Two unexpected findings:

- *Not one person mentioned the culture change effort as part of his work (results, tasks, decisions, obstacles, time allocation).*

- *Not one person mentioned innovation of any kind.*

As a result of these unexpected responses, the company decided to use the performance pipeline to communicate the required culture change as results to be delivered and to set the standard for those results for every leader around the world. Their original purpose was development, but based on what they discovered in the interviews, their primary purpose became performance.

I would encourage you, after analyzing the interview data, to reconsider what additional purpose, beyond the purpose(s) defined at the outset, is key to your organization's success. Aggregating all responses to the "obstacle" and the "need more authority" questions will give you a sense of where trouble spots exist, how pervasive they are, and where changes in current management practices are needed.

By Layer

With six to ten completed interviews for each layer in hand you can begin to build your performance pipeline. Start with Managers of Others (first-line managers) and follow these steps. A quick read of the example of an actual performance pipeline at the end of this book (Tool 1) will help you see where this is going.

Lessons Learned

All the data will give you an insider's view of what's really going on in the organization

I've found that people in Human Resources are astonished by the insights these interviews provide about who does what in the company. Analyzing the data gives clarity about challenges. Therefore, use the interview to learn the business. If you do enough of them, you will be the most knowledgeable person in your company about its inner workings.

Step 1

Read through one entire interview to get a feel for the person and how she sees her job in this layer.

Step 2

Pick out all the nouns, because they are results. Nouns such as *strategy*, *sales*, *teams*, *suppliers*, *expenses*, and *people* all provide "clues" as to what is important and needs to be spotlighted and measured in this position. It should be easy to do with questions 1, 2, 3A, 3B, and 4 (Tool 2). For questions like 5 and 6 you will have to interpret answers to understand what the "noun" is. *Team-building skills* means *team*; *time spent planning* means *plans*. Repeat this for each interview.

Step 3

Choose the work categories that suit your business or company. Every business needs operating or financial results, management results, leadership results, and relationship results. You may use other language or additional ideas for your categories. You can also create a category for addressing a special need.

Example—A Large Financial Services Company

- *Financial Results*

- *Customer Effectiveness Results (adding, serving, and keeping customers)*

- *Management Results*

- *Leadership Results*

- *Relationship Results*

- *Global Effectiveness Results (support for other geographies and businesses)*

Example—A Diversified Construction and Marine Products Company

- *Delivering Results*

- *Health, Safety, and Environment*

- *People and Teams*

- *Hands-on Management*

- *Customer Driven*

- *Open and Direct Dialogue*

Examples of Special Needs Categories Currently in Use

- *Growth Results*

- *Brand Delivery Results*

- *Innovation Results*

- *Safety Results*

- *Social Responsibility Results*

- *User/Patient Results (health care company)*

Step 4

Create column one ("Results") of the performance pipeline for this layer (see Tool 1). Fit all the nouns into the work categories you have chosen. Make a judgment about the adequacy of the list. Does this look right and sound right? Should some of these work elements be at a lower level? a higher level?

Step 5

Decide what work elements are missing from the list, and make any additions. Are there any important company initiatives that should be represented in some way? Are basic requirements like developing a successor, or executing the strategy, or improving business process adequately represented?

Refer to lists developed by other companies as displayed in the following chapters. In addition, note that the performance pipeline isn't meant to replace the planning process; it supplements it. Add the KPIs or goals as an attachment to the standards for each leader.

Step 6

Set the standards (column two, "Full Performance"). Now two critical decisions have to be made. First, where do you want to set the bar for performance? Is meeting budgeted objectives full performance or exceptional performance? How many new customers do you want to add? How many successors should each leader have? In many ways this is the hardest part to get right. Usually it is easier to lower a standard later than to raise it later.

Lessons Learned
The Performance Pipeline provides essential adaptability

One big reason that strategies fail is that new work required by the strategy isn't assigned to anyone or is assigned to only a few people. The Performance Pipeline enables regular reassessment of all standards and allows you to change them quickly as strategy changes. Changing the standards enables a conversation between a leader and her team about strategic direction, new priorities, a different way of working, and role clarity. Every leader can stay aware in a simple and straightforward way of new outcomes expected. Those role profiles or job descriptions you have been using just aren't adaptable without a lot of effort.

Second, determine the number of standards you will employ. Not all work elements need to have a standard. Not all work elements are critical every year. Choose the twenty to twenty-five most important work elements based on this year's operating plan and what you need to execute your strategy this year. Write standards for them. My rule of thumb for any company's first performance pipeline is fewer but high standards. Others can be added later.

Step 7

Define exceptional performance (column three). If exceptional performance isn't defined, full performance will soon be viewed as exceptional. For the Performance Pipeline, exceptional performance has three elements. First, results were substantially higher than plan or budget; a few percentage points higher isn't exceptional. You can trust your intuition on this. Second, exceptional performance is often the best amongst peers. It is or becomes the role model that others try to emulate. Third, exceptional performance can be something relevant but entirely new, or something no one has thought of in your company. Recognize, though, that not every full performance standard needs an exceptional counterpart. In fact some standards, like safety, don't fit any of the three exceptional elements. A year with no lost-time injuries or accidents is what's expected no matter what goal you set.

Step 8

Define the transition in work values. Work values (see Lessons Learned box on the following page) continue to be the sticking point in the upward movement of leaders and the main reason for performance that is not meeting requirements established for a given level. Leaders have to learn to value the work required at their new layer or existing layer.

Natural progressions exist that define the transition in work values. There are also some things that are unique and have to

Lessons Learned
When leaders move up but don't adopt the work values of their assigned layer, the business won't grow properly and the leaders don't develop

At lower passages, leaders must value, pursue, and deliver today's results. Included are such things as product delivery, customer satisfaction, and cost management. At upper passages, leaders must value, pursue, and deliver a definition of the future, investment for long-term payoff, development of future leaders, and cultivation of possible new partners. When leaders move up but continue to value, pursue, and deliver today's results, the business can't grow properly. Critical requirements for future success are not being delivered. Shifting work values is the underlying driver; not shifting work values becomes the underlying problem.

be thought through. What follows are two examples of natural progression of work values, first in achieving results, and second in the changes of time frame and content in planning:

Layer	Achieving Results—Using Organization, Not Just People
Self-Manager	Through own effort and collaborating with peers
Manager of Others	Through the work of others
Manager of Managers	Through managers (not through self-managers)
Function Manager	Through an entire function
Business Manager	Through integration of all functions
Group Manager	Through business managers
Enterprise Manager	Through integrated systems and processes

Layer	Planning—Important Changes in Time Frame and Content
Self-Manager	Project completion and weekly production
Manager of Others	Annual cycle for goals and budgets
Manager of Managers	Two-year operating plan
Function Manager	Three-to-five-year functional strategy
Business Manager	Five-year business strategy
Group Manager	Ten-year portfolio strategic framework
Enterprise Manager	Ten or more years enterprise strategic framework

The nature of your business drives many changes in work values required by layer. For example, some experts (Self-Managers) in financial services do business with the CEO and Chief Financial Officer in customer companies. They have to learn relationship-building for its own sake with very senior executives at companies that are not now but might become customers—they may need to transition from valuing relationships with current customers to valuing relationships with people in general (to create networks, alliances, friendships, partnerships, and so on). Thinking through the point of contact and the nature of the relationship is the starting point. Thinking through the broadening of contacts is also important. In this way, people can reflect on what types of relationship they value (and what types of relationship they ignore but need to value). Leaders, for instance, need to consider community relationships; at what layer do a majority of leaders get involved in the community?

Step 9

Decide what else to include in your performance pipeline. Required changes in work values should be at the top of the page (see Tool 1). If the first column contains the work elements, the second column lists the full performance standards, and the third lists the exceptional performance standards, what do you need in the fourth column? Most companies choose to identify the skills, experience, and knowledge required to do the job (see Tool 1, column four). These are extremely useful for planning development, coaching, and diagnosing problems. It is well worth the time required to produce this list. Clear direction is thus provided to everyone who wants to improve his performance.

Several companies have chosen to fit their competency models here. That's a great idea because the competencies originally were created to help produce results, although the connection between competencies and results has been lost in most cases. Inserting competency models into the fourth column can help restore that connection.

Column four can be used too to spell out what you *don't* want:

Example

A major software firm felt that their managers needed additional guidance from the organization. They decided to use the fourth column to identify the signs that conveyed inappropriate performance or poor transition to the layer. For a Manager of Others, column four included: "spends all his time in his office with the door closed" and "solves all the hard problems himself." That idea may be useful to you if your company is new and growing very fast, or if you have not yet built a management culture in your company, or if you are trying to change management practices.

Validating the Standards

Before your newly minted performance pipeline is put into practice, interviewees and senior management should review it. Conducting validation sessions with groups of people rather than individually seems to work best. The give-and-take in the room helps everyone get calibrated on performance and enables a common definition of key words.

Allowing Some Flexibility

How your performance pipeline gets used is a matter of choice based on your current needs and your feelings about what your people can absorb. Some companies have suggested that measuring their leaders on twenty-five standards instead of their five or six KPIs or goals was too much to ask. So, they used their performance pipeline for leadership development only, at least in the first year of its use. Their rationale was that the concept needed to be socialized before it was implemented.

Several companies have used their performance pipeline initially to improve succession planning. In-depth definitions of each

---

Lessons Learned

Validation meetings provide increased specificity to roles

Without validation meetings, dialogue about roles—both of participants in the meetings and of direct reports and supervisors—rarely happens. Most leaders have some level of concern about their own role and about what they should be asking of their direct reports. Despite instructions that request some standards be eliminated so that the document can be tight and focused, every single validation group in my experience has added standards! They want more specificity, not less.

Good facilitation is required to keep validation meetings on track. Don't try to solve all the company's problems in this setting. A scribe is also needed to record the changes and additions. True ownership can be achieved in a robust meeting, so every effort should be made to utilize participants' suggested changes. Obviously, some editing by a knowledgeable person will be required.

---

layer improved consistency and precision for both performance and potential ratings. Development plans for improving performance and enhancing potential were grounded in more substantial targets. Succession planning can't be effective if you lack a performance pipeline that is specific to the company. In fact, one CEO told me, "I don't know how we ever did succession planning without this definition."

Of course, some companies have used the Pipeline model for performance measurement right away and found it to be extraordinarily useful. We'll look at how the performance management process is changed by the Performance Pipeline, and how to get maximum value from it, in Chapter Eleven.

Company E's performance is a good example of the most commonly used version of a performance pipeline. It is displayed as Tool 1—an actual performance pipeline—at the end of this book. Look carefully at the transition in work values listed at the top of the first page for each layer. The content in all four columns is classic.

Lessons Learned
Operating management will grab the Performance Pipeline and run with it even if Human Resources isn't ready to put it into practice

Leaders in operational roles tend to grasp the Pipeline's value immediately and want to use it right now for performance management, succession planning, organization, and coaching. At the software company that built its column four around examples of inappropriate or incomplete performance, the software engineering leaders grabbed the performance standards and started using them immediately despite implementation concerns and well in advance of HR's planned rollout.

Since the CEO is a single position with unique requirements, I don't usually write performance standards for that position, and the companies haven't requested them. A unique definition for this unique role seems to make more sense. For this reason, there is no Enterprise Manager layer in Tool 1. Results, though, should be defined for CEOs even if standards aren't created.

The next seven chapters will cover the results that should be delivered at each layer, starting with the Enterprise CEO and working down the Performance Pipeline. Each chapter provides specific definitions of results to be delivered at that layer and the enablers to be passed down to the layer below in order to make it successful. I recommend that you read each chapter before attempting to build your own performance standards for that layer.

Part II

Expected Results at Every Level of Leadership

2

Enterprise Chief Executive Officer
Perpetuating the Enterprise

What should an Enterprise CEO contribute to the enterprise? What results should he or she be judged on? What should others in the enterprise count on from their CEO?

Many companies answer these questions much too narrowly. From thirty years of working with CEOs and their teams and developing over forty CEO succession plans, I know that many misconceptions exist as to a CEO's contributions. Media perspectives especially distort expectations for CEO performance. Boards of Directors are ever more active and demand more attention on a few critical results. An uncertain environment commands attention and study. Customers are more demanding. Financial markets and analysts are relentlessly questioning and challenging. As a result there is tremendous pressure on the CEO to focus upward and outward. *The pendulum has swung toward externals, and the internal needs are not being sufficiently addressed.*

Most CEOs seem to know they can't succeed without a great team, sound strategies, and an organization that can execute. Building and maintaining these also takes time and attention. CEOs have to strike the right balance in their performance between external and internal needs. Understanding the nature of their internal impact on results at all leadership levels is essential. If we get the results requirements for CEOs wrong, the entire performance pipeline is compromised. By targeting the right results for CEOs, we ensure that they're doing their jobs the best way possible rather than doing the jobs of people at other levels in the worst way possible.

(It is now common to call people who run a business "CEO," which adds to the confusion. This chapter is about Enterprise CEOs: what they should contribute and what they must pass down to make others, and the enterprise, successful.)

Example

When Larry took over as CEO of a struggling transportation business, he inherited some good leaders, an experienced workforce, and very strong market positions in two businesses. However, the problems greatly outnumbered the strengths. The company was not as profitable as it should be, in part because there wasn't enough focus on serving the customer. Long-standing silos made teamwork nonexistent. Corporate Staff Functions had too much power. One Business Group had more losing businesses than profitable businesses. At middle management layers—the Function Managers and the Managers of Managers—most leaders lacked a sense of accountability and focused primarily on their technical work. Firefighting and maintaining the status quo were the norm, not driving needed change in customer service and cost management. Perhaps the most troubling situation was the absence of accurate and timely financial data, resulting in painful business decision making. The company was also short-staffed (Larry lacked a CFO, and two Business Groups had only acting leaders), and it was overly dependent on temporary employees. On top of all this, the company had alarming safety issues—a serious accident had occurred days after his arrival.

Making it his mission to learn about the company, Larry started by visiting key customers. Then, after touring the company, addressing both large and small employee gatherings and listening to people at every level, he stepped back. He had been bombarded with ideas, complaints, excuses, and the like. He had to make some tough decisions about priorities and his own contribution.

Larry determined that safety would be his number one priority, followed by customer service and commercial success. He helped fill open positions reporting to him with capable new recruits who could run their own Corporate Staff Function or Business Group. He did not try to run the businesses or staff functions. Larry had the newly hired CFO drive improvement in data accuracy and enhance the commercial thinking in capital investment decisions. Larry also challenged the new leaders of Business Groups to improve their results in areas such as on-time service, cost control, and profitability.

Bringing in the world's leading safety consulting company to provide advice, Larry spoke with almost all employees about making safety their number one priority. Well aware of the threats facing the enterprise, Larry implemented new training for everyone in safety practices, added new measures, and overhauled communication procedures.

Larry also addressed employee accountability for serving customers and for producing improved results. A five-pillar strategic framework set the overall direction that Larry wanted. He helped create a performance pipeline to define the expected results for every leader. Safety was at the top of the results list, but customer service received considerable attention as did commercial success. He challenged all leaders to improve the capability of their teams and to develop successors.

Focusing on feedback and coaching, Larry held monthly one-on-one meetings with his direct reports. As he worked to build the enterprise's ability to be safe and to deliver service, he also developed each senior leader's ability to perform. He chose to focus on results that affect all customers and all employees while giving his direct reports direction and room to operate so that they could build their businesses and functions.

After three years in the job, Larry has been successful by any measure. Results have been strong enough to enable a successful IPO. Larry chose to do several things that should be done by new Enterprise CEOs. He

- *Took time to think through the long-term requirements of his job, not just pursue short-term wins*

- *Focused on big challenges that involve and affect everyone, not just Marketing or Operations improvements*

- *Installed a performance pipeline that gave every leader new marching orders and standards that clarified expectations*

- *Gave his direct reports space to do their jobs and the coaching needed to improve their skills*

- *Added some new talent as a first priority without demeaning those already in place*

- *Listened to the organization and to the customs, not just the customer*

Although he had never been an Enterprise CEO, Larry knew it was a job he wanted and he paid attention to his development along the way. It was clear to him from his observations and readings that the enterprise is just one thing, like a basketball, not a collection of things, like a bagful of golf balls.

What a CEO Must Produce

The CEO's purpose is to perpetuate the enterprise. He puts in place those things that will keep the enterprise successful for as long as possible. A handful of critical results seems to make the most difference: earnings, a high-functioning team at the top of the enterprise, a strategic framework, a performance pipeline, high-level external relationships, talent, a healthy brand, and an "immune system." The job is bigger than these, of course, so other important results will be spelled out here as well. Pay particular attention to these critical results, however, as you read this chapter. Results that drive the enterprise toward a successful future can be categorized for the CEO in the same way as in positions at lower levels in the enterprise. These categories are

- Business Results—financial and customer outcomes

- Leadership Results—the human side of business

- Management Results—planning, organizing, integrating, measuring, executing

- Relationship Results—the necessary connections

- Innovation Results—new ways to add value

When you consider all these results, what's surprising is that CEOs *produce* very few of them compared to the large number of results they *enable* others to produce. This enabling portion of the CEO's requirements is where much of the confusion arises about a CEO's contribution. This is especially true in large companies that do business around the world and in those with diverse business units. CEOs often leave the enabling results to others because they are busy appearing at glamorous events and attending to powerful people. They have little or no time for making lower levels successful.

The following sections will take a close look at the five main types of results mentioned in our list here. (I won't be discussing some important categories of results like Social Responsibility or Global Effectiveness because they are too company-specific.) As we examine these five types, I'm going to focus both on the most significant results CEOs deliver themselves and on the results they enable others to achieve. What many people find interesting is the way widely accepted CEO results are actually derived from critically important *underlying* results. These underlying results are also real requirements for CEO effectiveness and must be understood and delivered. The following sections will make clear what the underlying results are and why they are important.

Business Results

Some companies and CEOs prefer to call this category "Operating Results" and establish separate categories for things like Brand Delivery or Customer Results; but for our purposes, these will be included under "Business Results." Let's look at what these results entail.

Earnings, Earnings per Share, Profit

Tremendous pressure is placed on the CEO to deliver earnings in exactly the amount forecasted or risk losing huge amounts of market capitalization. Earnings matter not just to the CEO, of course, but also to investors, owners, shareholders, and the Board of Directors. Earnings are the result of a wide range of actions, decisions, plans, execution steps, and the like. Though other leaders and employees impact earnings, CEOs contribute in two ways. First, they *learn* what the organization can do and what market conditions are likely to be. Second, and on the basis of this learning, they set appropriate *targets*. These targets focus everyone's efforts. These underlying results—learning and targets—make a major difference.

Recall our discussion of uncertainties in the Introduction; each one of those uncertainties impacts the CEO's contribution in this area of earnings. To deal effectively with all the question marks that exist, CEOs must invite others into the process and build a team at the top. Honest information, thoughtful research, realistic assessments of the organization's capability, candid feedback, validated assumptions, and well-founded projections are all needed. CEOs also must choose the right people to help them. For instance, they must make sure that an individual is motivated to contribute in the best interests of the enterprise, and not just in his own self-interest. People who make it to the top usually have very strong egos and considerable personal ambition. Choosing them carefully for their ability to be a team player is critical.

To set the right earnings targets, CEOs have a range of internal responsibilities: strategies that deliver the right positioning of the business, operating plans that define how profit will be achieved, and so on. These internal requirements are tough, but they are within the enterprise's control. An equal number of external variables, however, are much more difficult to control.

Outside the enterprise, CEOs must establish a wide range of connections and relationships. In fact, CEOs are often the only people who can make these connections—with leaders of customer companies, supplier companies, government at local and national levels, nongovernmental organizations (NGOs), and with partners and key investors.

Therefore, the results required for earnings, earnings per share, or profits are extensive. Great CEOs don't deliver great earnings just by focusing on the financials, however. To understand the real story behind their contributions to earnings, consider what CEOs deliver and what they enable in this area:

What the CEO delivers

- Earnings targets that are demanding but attainable
- A team to support the decision making

- Data processes that produce accurate information

- Strategies, operating plans, and budgets that define how profit will be achieved and sustained

- Relationships with those on the critical path

What the CEO enables

- Candid communication of the targets for earnings, earnings per share, and profit

- A context for performance that gets the best from everyone

- Long-term and short-term understanding of profit needs

While people tend to judge CEOs on profit figures, these underlying results and enabling results provide a more accurate description of how their performance impacts the enterprise in the short and long term, and how profit happens.

Customers

CEOs sometimes take on too much customer responsibility, especially when they come up through the Sales and Marketing tracks. CEOs have a role to play here, but it shouldn't usurp the power or accountability of Sales and Marketing or their business leader. Perhaps the biggest mistake CEOs make in this area is offering concessions that serve as "deal sweeteners." In other words, they use their visits to show customers how committed they are by lowering pricing or improving terms. Unfortunately, this often results in customers refusing to take any actions in the future without a visit from the CEO first.

It is a rare CEO who doesn't want to meet with customers. CEOs must, however, establish the purpose for such visits. Building a future-oriented partnership or relationship adds great value. Strategizing together, planning together, getting personal commitments for delivery, communicating mutual support—these are all examples of what can be done without jeopardizing the work of Sales and Marketing. Obviously, legal and ethical standards must be followed along with transparency requirements.

What the CEO delivers

- Senior-level customer relationships that enable good business

What the CEO enables

- Information about the future as the customer sees it

- Acceptance of the enterprise's products and services by customers

Brand

Here the challenge for CEOs is to set or reset the brand standard without becoming overly involved in the brand-building work. Preserving and enhancing the enterprise's brand identity is a high priority with most CEOs. For new or changing companies, defining the brand can be the main requirement. Every CEO is accountable for the state of the brand when she leaves office. Great service or unpredictable service, high quality products or questionable products, safe working conditions or hazardous work conditions, being an employer of choice or a sweatshop are a few of the polarities of brand identity. The key thing CEOs need to keep in mind, though, is that brands are actually delivered by people working at much lower levels in the organization.

What the CEO delivers

- Clearly defined brand standards

What the CEO enables

- Sufficient resources to deliver the brand's promise

- Clear understanding of the brand requirements by all employees

- A disciplined work environment that supports brand building

Investment

Deciding where to invest, when to invest, how much to invest, and where, when, and how *not* to invest are frequent challenges for any CEO. Starting at the right place is what helps CEOs make meaningful contributions in this area. The right place is a clear picture of the desired future state, both near term and long term. Effective CEOs define the future they want and start pulling it into the present by investing in areas of future importance. The investment could be as simple as new equipment or as complicated as a new business. Risk-averse CEOs who are reluctant to invest in the future get caught short at the worst possible time.

What the CEO delivers

- Investment decisions that fit and enable the vision or strategy

What the CEO enables

- Future state definition

- Commitment to the future

Getting at the underlying Business Results helps both the CEO and all employees—particularly those who participate in the decision-making process—get clarity about the business and focus on the appropriate components of profit. Missing profit targets by only a penny or two can cost billions in market capitalization. Delivering promised Business Results over and over is the proof that this enterprise will survive.

Leadership Results

Leadership Results are often poorly defined for CEOs, producing substandard performance. To define Leadership Results effectively for CEOs, we need to look at three areas: the direction the enterprise should take; engagement with employees to get their participation and buy-in; and enabling success by taking needed actions, including acquiring resources. All of this is easier to do if the right talent is on board.

Direction—The Strategic Framework

Setting the direction for the organization is every leader's first priority, but it is especially important for the CEO. Direction can take many forms, including vision, mission, values, enterprise strategic framework, business strategy, operating plans, budgets, goals, a balanced scorecard, and key performance indicators. CEOs usually focus on the first few, depending on the company's size and maturity. Vision, mission, and values are normally part of what CEOs must deliver. Founders usually establish those three, and they usually have a long life, but they may need updating and revising for the current business reality. While others may assist CEOs in defining these things, CEOs have to do the heavy lifting.

CEOs must establish an enterprise strategic framework for pulling together all the energy and effort generated in pursuit of the vision and mission. This framework sets the boundaries for the company and includes things like context for performance (discussed in Chapter Nine), the performance pipeline, the strategic playing field that those below need for developing portfolio strategy or business strategy, and the social architecture that governs day-to-day behavior. Usually, the strategic framework includes all of these interwoven elements.

Since enterprises come in many different shapes and sizes, not all CEO positions are the same. In large enterprises where many business units are managed by Group Managers, the CEO doesn't develop portfolio strategy or business strategy. In enterprises where several businesses report directly to the CEO, the CEO develops the portfolio strategy. In single-business enterprises the CEO creates business strategy and portfolio strategy.

What the CEO delivers

- Vision, mission, values (new or updated)

- Enterprise strategic framework clear enough to penetrate the clutter

What the CEO enables

- Guidance for everyone's effort and energy

- Portfolio strategy and business strategy

- Sense of purpose for everyone

Clear and consistent direction, in many ways, is the single most important result that a CEO delivers.

Engagement

Face-to-face discussions about the enterprise's direction is a key CEO responsibility. CEOs sell the logic and establish the need for their choice of direction, and they do so for as many employees as possible. They must tell the story, but they must also make the effort to hear the response; they should pay special attention to problems with acceptance or to strong opposing beliefs. The audience may well have information and experience that the CEO lacks. The purpose of engagement is understanding and accep-tance. Getting understanding may take several discussions. Gaining acceptance may require some redefinition of or adjustment to the direction.

As time passes and assumptions prove to be correct or incorrect, new engagement must take place. Employees at all levels may lose confidence in the chosen direction. They may also have ideas about how to get there faster, cheaper, better. New employees may not be sufficiently informed or may have useful new insights. One bold engagement to sell the direction just isn't enough.

What the CEO delivers

- Clarity and reason (for the direction)
- Redirection when circumstances warrant it

What the CEO enables

- Understanding and acceptance of the direction by all employees
- Conviction and commitment to the direction
- One direction for everyone
- A focus on what is important
- Free flow of information and ideas
- Commitment from people the CEO may never see

Facilitation

CEOs must convince their people that they're serious about the direction they set, and the best way to accomplish this objective is by helping people overcome the obstacles they face, obtain the resources they need, and acquire the capabilities that are missing—all of these issues surface during the engagement process. By investing in training and development, in the acquisition of new people with the necessary skills, and in the removal of obstacles that prevent people from delivering expected results, CEOs facilitate a belief in the enterprise's success and the success of individuals. The workforce has to believe that pursuing the defined path is possible, not just a CEO fantasy.

What the CEO delivers

- The money for needed resources and capability

- Understanding of the challenge

What the CEO enables

- Acquisition of needed resources

- Belief in the direction

- Capability to achieve the direction

- Success in pursuing the direction

The facilitation process is the real difference between wishing the enterprise will succeed and making it possible for the enterprise to succeed.

Senior Talent

The CEO has the unique requirement of looking after those individuals considered to be "corporate property." This includes his successor, his direct reports, their direct reports, and likely successors to the two layers below him. At a minimum, corporate property includes everyone responsible for delivering profit (a bottom line) and successors to those positions. Assuring the board and other key stakeholders that the enterprise can staff these positions quickly and with high confidence is one ingredient for ensuring perpetuation of the enterprise. CEOs who get involved in the appointments to those key positions, the development of the incumbents and their successors, reassignments, job changes, and career discussions have a much better sense of these leaders' capabilities. Ensuring that difficult reassignments get made that test key people in new roles with new bosses has proven to be of great value. It is something only the CEO can do. An effective CEO produces a workforce and, in particular, leaders that are committed to perpetuating the enterprise because they see that the enterprise leader cares about them.

Management Results

Management is getting a "bad rap" these days. It is equated with bureaucracy, viewed as stifling innovation, and considered an old idea in a new world. But it's not management that's the problem; it's poor management. CEOs who take good management seriously do so by focusing on plans, organization, and control mechanisms that underpin effective execution. They also build and maintain a performance pipeline.

Plans

Plans are the necessary follow-on to the established direction, engagement, and facilitation. Highly motivated and committed leaders and other employees can't just be "turned loose." Priorities, cost limits, manpower, and other new resources have to be aligned. Most CEOs don't do planning themselves. Instead, they request their direct reports to prepare plans that are focused on delivering the strategy in an orderly way including acceptable goals and budgets. Reviews of plans developed by others to ensure strategic fit and alignment are the tasks. Approval is the result.

What the CEO delivers

- Planning parameters or guidelines

- Timely final approval (permission to proceed)

What the CEO enables

- Requests for planning submissions that have the CEO's authority

- Planning infrastructure

- Plans—strategies, operating plans, tactical plans

Organization

The organization structure provides the connection for each employee to the strategies and plans. Specific assignments for individuals that add up to all the results is the challenge. CEOs define the overall enterprise organization structure, including Corporate Staff and Operating Units that report to them. That definition has a major impact on what performance will be achieved. Corporate Staff Functions are relatively straightforward. CEOs, though, have to give more thought to whether the functions will be combined under a Chief Administrative Officer (or some variation), or all report directly to the CEO, or be combined for some and direct for others. CEOs' requests define what is expected from the Corporate Staff, since the CEO is their primary and sometimes sole focus.

On the operating side, the CEO makes the structural choice of groups of business units or individual business units, or functions as direct reports. Other choices include geography, customers, products, or problems. Operating structure decisions have a huge impact on how the enterprise will work. The usual deciding factor is the alignment with strategy—that is, which structure will best deliver the strategy?

Performance Pipeline Effectiveness

The vertical organization structure has many more possibilities than the horizontal structure and provides flow and connectivity up and down that the horizontal doesn't. The CEO sits at the very top of the performance pipeline and is the only leader with easy access to all of it. She is the logical person to own it. Free flow downward of work and information requires the right connections between the layers. Cost management and leadership development require the right work to be done at the right level. Building speed and efficiency requires a complete understanding of how the Performance Pipeline works, where the pinch points might be, where confusion comes from, and where decisions are made. From this ownership, she knows exactly how this company makes money, adds value, satisfies customers, or fails to deliver.

CEOs can commission building the performance pipeline by others but must validate the performance standards themselves. Regular discussions with people at every layer to find out what they are getting done and what's in their way provide the best picture of how the enterprise really works. CEOs learn how their enterprise actually makes money so they don't have to guess. They also learn quickly who the good leaders are, the ones to whom they can entrust decision-making authority.

What the CEO delivers

- An enterprise organization structure that can deliver the strategy

- A performance pipeline ensuring that all work is assigned

- Process requirements and process discipline

- Standards for staffing and effective staffing decisions

- Power distribution to appropriate levels

What the CEO enables

- Corporate policy

- Proper connection of the layers

- Practices that enforce process discipline

- Decisions made at the appropriate level

- Who can be on the payroll and who can't

Controls and an Immune System

CEOs have to control from the front, middle, and back. Stopping problems before they start, heading off trouble before it impacts the enterprise, is the one truly effective control system. The corporate strategic framework, the performance pipeline, and vision, mission, and values are mechanisms for controlling from the front. Everyone gets a sense of direction and purpose before taking action.

Keeping all the work on track and meeting all delivery dates at the right cost and quality is an enormous task that requires controlling from the middle, that is, controlling while work is in progress. CEOs have a major role to play both personally and through enabling others. They must establish regular reviews with their direct reports, individually and collectively. Weekly staff meetings, one-on-one discussion, and regular reporting are standard in many companies. Walking around, site visits, and special events are also common. When the enterprise has too many transactions on a daily basis for the CEO to review or too many people for the CEO to see, additional control mechanisms are needed.

Building an enterprise "immune system" is becoming more and more common. The Finance and Human Resource staff are used as extensions of the CEO down to the bottom of the organization. They have responsibility for stopping inappropriate transactions on the spot. If the offending person doesn't respond, the Finance or Human Resource person has the right to evaluate the problem until an appropriate response is delivered. Things like inappropriate hiring decisions, reporting false or erroneous information, and withholding important facts are examples of the "viruses" the immune system addresses.

Timely and frequent financial reporting at all levels is probably the best form of controlling from the back. Discussion that is open and candid makes timely corrections possible.

What the CEO delivers

- Clear direction with standards
- An immune system
- Regular reviews of all kinds
- Frequent feedback to direct reports and others as appropriate

What the CEO enables

- Audits of all kinds
- Candid and frequent feedback at all levels
- A climate of commitment to results
- Free flow of performance information
- Strategy revisions (when appropriate)

By using the performance pipeline and good management practices, the CEO has enormous power for driving results at all levels.

Relationship Results

Most CEOs recognize that they are responsible for connecting the enterprise to the world around it. Some of the relationships that arise from this connecting process are obvious, such as those with government leaders, heads of customer and supplier organizations, industry leaders, and investors. Some aren't so obvious, including those with thought leaders, CEOs from parallel industries, and people who can give business advice. In all cases, the relationships should accomplish two primary objectives: help the flow of information in and out that may help both sides, and establish trust in the enterprise by external stakeholders. In terms of this second objective, people should feel that CEOs can be trusted to do the right thing at all times but especially under pressure.

Internal relationships cannot be assumed. The trust and confidence of those who work in the enterprise isn't easy to obtain and requires continuous effort to maintain. Engagement has already been discussed under Leadership Results, but it is worth repeating. Employees need to see and hear the CEO in order to know what she stands for. Too many CEOs are strangers to their own people while being fully engaged externally.

Each Board of Directors has unique requirements that the CEO must address. Boards are both critics and advisors. Their confidence in the CEO produces benefits like speed of decision making, acceptance of strategy changes, and approval of investment requests. Striking a balance in the amount of attention given to the board in order to win its confidence requires thoughtful planning by the CEO. Overdoing it is as bad as under-doing it.

What the CEO delivers

- Trust and confidence within the enterprise

- Broad external relationship base

- Board of Directors' confidence and support

What the CEO enables

- Acceptance of the enterprise by externals

- Access to information and other resources

- Positive environment for internal relationships

Relationships are a great enabler, and CEOs must build them in all directions if they are to deliver their results.

Innovation Results

Perpetuating the enterprise requires adaptation to a changing environment. The CEO's long-term success is tied directly to his ability to innovate, to add value in new ways for customers, and to satisfy the changing needs of stakeholders. Actual innovation takes place at lower levels, but an effective CEO makes expectations clear and execution possible. Innovations can be big (inventions) or small (process improvements), but they need facilitating.

Clear Expectations

Every employee can be innovative if he knows it is expected. CEOs help this happen by establishing clear expectations and consistently communicating those expectations, setting standards, and measuring results. Innovating requires extra thought and extra effort, which may not happen without a forcing function. The performance pipeline is being used today to convey both expectations and measurements. What seems to work best is making the requirements clear without specifying the nature of the innovation. That can be specified by lower levels of management with more precision.

Support for Execution

CEOs have more ways to support innovation than anyone else in the enterprise. Budgets, awards, organization, publicity, and recognition are just some of the choices. What matters here is that the choices be credible and convincing. Setting a climate that encourages learning and experimentation without punishing mistakes is one of the best choices. This subject is big enough to have entire books written about it. The intent here is to create awareness, not provide all the answers.

What the CEO delivers

- Clear expectations for innovation

- Standards for measurement

- Supportive climate

- Rewards and recognition

What the CEO enables

- Full participation

- Willingness to try

- Local management and application

What CEOs Must Not Produce

The CEO's primary role is to perpetuate the enterprise, to make sure the enterprise is successful. That leaves little time for working on extraneous or counterproductive results. So, we don't want CEOs delivering the following:

All the answers. As CEOs become more and more effective in their role, those who report to them, and frequently many at lower layers, want to know what the CEO thinks, what the CEO wants, what the CEO would do. Many decisions or questions are thus deferred to him. While it is seductive to have one's opinion or judgment sought on almost everything, giving it will destroy the organization. It creates too much dependence and eliminates even reasonable challenge. People stop doing the necessary research and analysis when the CEO has all the answers.

All the power. Far too many people believe plans, projects, programs, changes, and the like need the CEO's backing in order to be successful. While the CEO should know what new initiatives are being planned and implemented, he should not have to empower them. Conscious and specific delegation of authority and the deliberate empowering of key people below him require constant reinforcement. The entire organization needs to know that Group Executives, Corporate Function Heads, and other key leaders speak with his authority.

Emotional decisions. Passion is in vogue as a worthwhile ingredient for everyone but especially for leaders. It comes up as a key ingredient for success in companies all over the world. While it is useful at several organization levels, particularly for those who directly make the product or serve customers, it is poison for a CEO. Dispassionate decision making is much more useful. Analyzing what works and what doesn't, being ready to abandon practices that used to be important but don't work now, and balancing the interests of all stakeholders are what CEOs need, not the imbalance that comes from passion.

Finding the Right Balance

When it comes to results at the top of the organization, CEOs must strike a delicate balance. Focusing their efforts too narrowly causes everyone else in the enterprise to be shortchanged in some way; focusing too broadly can rob others of initiative. Delivering results, too, is only one part of the equation. Understanding what must be enabled is worth whatever effort is required. If you are a CEO, if you work with a CEO, or if you give guidance to CEOs, understanding the enabling factors I've listed in each results category in this chapter should be among the highest priorities. Too many CEOs become enmeshed in the glamour and power associated with their positions, and they lose sight of their obligation to make the enterprise successful. Delivering results while enabling others to succeed requires maturity as well as balance and owning the performance pipeline. So many CEOs have overemphasized the external parts of their job that the internal parts are being neglected. Our uncertain business climate makes that imbalance worse. Finding the right balance between external and internal concerns is tougher than ever. Achieving the CEO's purpose—perpetuation of the enterprise—requires sustained and sustainable results produced by the entire workforce. Thinking beyond themselves and their tenure helps CEOs succeed; making everyone successful helps the enterprise live on.

3

Group Managers
Portfolio of Businesses

et's start out by defining the Group Manager layer, since definitions can vary by organization and industry. A Group Manager
is accountable for several businesses and may be called Group
CEO, Region Executive, or Sector Executive. Some smaller companies have only one Group Manager; she might be the President
or Chief Operating Officer. Group Managers are responsible for
delivering the portfolio strategy, which includes deciding what
businesses the enterprise should embrace and what businesses
should be abandoned. They must also build succession to the
Business Manager layer to be sure qualified people exist to run the
businesses. I'll go into more depth about these two key contributions as well some others that may not be so obvious but are
nonetheless significant.

First, though, let me share two insights about Group Managers
that have emerged from my work. Because Group Managers are
the primary candidates for CEO, I have been closely involved with
many of them in my CEO succession assignments.

Of all the senior executive positions, this one is in greatest need
of role clarity and focus. All too frequently, Group Managers
meddle in the businesses under them for want of a clear purpose.

Don't create Group Manager positions simply because you lack
them, but do make sure specific executives are accountable for this
layer's contributions. Many companies don't have Group Managers.
In those cases, leaders who report to the CEO must be accountable

for the results identified in this chapter. The needed results are core requirements and must be picked up by others. Decide who will pick up the accountability and consider the CEO as one candidate; consider too how to redistribute results responsibilities—topics I'll delve into later in the chapter.

The Most Overlooked Results for Group Managers

Example

During one week, the CEOs of three major US corporations independently asked me the same question: "How do I get my direct reports to sit around the table and talk about the company?" Those CEOs felt that the Group Managers just wanted to talk about and work their own businesses, their own budgets, their own needs.

Working with these three CEOs (separately), we discovered that Group Managers were not assuming responsibility for making the enterprise successful. Too much time was spent squabbling about resource allocation and priorities. Group Managers didn't support corporate initiatives and turned the CEO into a referee. The Corporate Function leaders—the Chief Financial Officer, Chief Human Resource Officer, Chief Legal Counsel, and so on—also reported to the CEO and also fell short in this results category. They were suboptimizing Enterprise Results by focusing only on the success of their function.

Accountability for Enterprise Results

Delivering Enterprise Financial Results is the first and most important result. That Group Executive should not be considered successful if he meets his targets but the enterprise doesn't. If a Group Manager delivers his own numbers but the enterprise misses its earnings targets, or important enterprise initiatives fail, bad publicity is likely and the share price can fall. Everyone at this layer has to pitch in, make adjustments to his own plans, share resources, and support company-wide initiatives.

Support for corporate initiatives is another key requirement for Group Managers—one that is often given a low priority or ignored altogether. Corporate Functions have results to deliver that span the enterprise. Once thoroughly discussed with the Group Managers and other Corporate Function Managers and approved by the CEO, these functional results become an obligation for the Group Manager. New financial reporting requirements, a new performance appraisal program, or a change in contract terms when fully reviewed by all peers and agreed to by the CEO need to be delivered. No matter how "burdened" the Group Manager feels, delivering corporate programs is a requirement. Group Managers must assume responsibility for their success in the group and across the company, even if they disagree with an initiative.

Conversely, Corporate Function Leaders must design programs, develop strategies, and design initiatives with a clear sense of their own accountability for Enterprise Results. This means both financial and nonfinancial results. Reasonable cost, ease of implementation, and impact on profit are required design criteria for corporate initiatives. Group Managers and Corporate Function Leaders have more required results in common than not. Teamwork at their level is critically important but rarely achieved. As productive as the creative tension between these two leadership groups can be, a supportive approach is even more productive.

Effective Capital Allocation

While profit is the responsibility of the Business Manager (one layer down), the Group Manager approves profit targets, makes resource trade-offs, and supports other adjustments to ensure total success. As part of this financial responsibility, Group Managers must master the intricacies of capital allocation. This type of result can be challenging, since deciding which business has the strategy with the greatest probability of success requires hard work and keen judgment. Since Group Managers have direct oversight of the strategies for each business, they have the best perspective for prioritizing capital allocations. They also have responsibility for deciding on new businesses to enter, and how to enter. Serious investment is usually required, so they must address additional investment priorities that emerge. On top of all this, they must be able to work closely with the Chief Financial Officer and other Group Managers to make astute allocation decisions and garner support for them. While the CEO and CFO deliver the total capital allocation strategy, Group Managers make the choices that impact larger enterprise decisions. When there aren't any Group Managers, the CEO and CFO make the capital allocation decisions with input from the CEO's team, the Business Managers, and other Corporate Staff Function Heads.

Environmental Scans and Tracking the Strategic Uncertainties

Because Group Managers don't run day-to-day businesses, they usually have time to scan the business horizon to check on competition, to assess industry trends, and to monitor the global economy. Thus, they can produce an analysis of the environment that enables Business Managers to make better decisions. They also enable a seldom discussed but badly needed scan of strategic uncertainties. Group Managers produce a portfolio strategy and then monitor the things that threaten their strategy. Actions taken or planned by competitors, governments, customers, unions, and others pose direct threats. Group Managers fail to enable this set of results when they take their eye off the ball. If they overlook threatening actions and fail to take corrective actions on a timely basis, their portfolio strategy will fall short. If they keep tracking these uncertainties and threats, however, then their analyses and likely decisions can be passed down to the Business Managers to help them make timely adjustments to business strategies.

What the Group Manager must deliver

- Enterprise Financial Results
- Group Financial Results
- Success of corporate initiatives
- Capital allocation recommendations
- Environmental scans
- Strategic uncertainty scans

What the Group Manager enables

- Capital for investment in businesses
- Environmental scans relevant to the businesses
- Strategic uncertainty assessments
- Timely adjustments to business strategies
- Acceptance of corporate initiatives

The Whole Job

Other Business Results: New Ventures

Building future business capability through new ventures, joint ventures, and partnerships is commonly part of the Group Manager's responsibilities. Finding ways to accelerate the development of new capability in response to changing conditions is more important now than ever. Since sharing technology, intellectual property, or other assets is common, choosing partners wisely or choosing to go it alone are major decisions.

Leadership Results

As important as Business Results are for Group Managers, the managers who are able to achieve future-oriented Leadership

Results are the most successful and are the best partners for the CEO. Strategy and people development are the biggest contributions, with enterprise leadership close on their heels—the enterprise's future rests on meeting profit projections, achieved by being in the right businesses at the right time with the right business leader and team.

Strategy

Strategy at this level means *portfolio* strategy. It defines the businesses that the enterprise should be in five to ten years from now. The trap for Group Managers from a performance standpoint: falling in love with the current businesses. Taking heroic actions to "save" a business may be acceptable if there is truly sustainable competitive advantage, but Group Managers shouldn't fool themselves or others. The managers who deliver Strategic Results learn to tell the difference between a business with a great future and a business with only a great past.

Strategic work at this level has the luxury of broad choices and the obligation to focus on real opportunity within the corporate strategic framework. Group Managers who shine find the market opportunities and figure out how to capture them in a sustainable way. They resist the temptation to wrestle with today's business problems, leaving them to the Business Managers. While Group Managers do have to reallocate resources from one business to another to ensure group success, they don't have to become bogged down solving problems in other areas. In fact, spending more time solving problems than pursuing opportunities is a red flag signaling that Group Managers are going after the wrong results. Finding opportunity in all this uncertainty is what their focus should be.

Portfolio strategy helps Business Managers see the shape of the likely future. It also helps these managers understand the enterprise strategic framework. When Group Managers make the portfolio strategy clear, the business strategies are more likely to be on target. Review and approval of the Business Manager's strategy are part of the Group Manager's requirements. An approved business strategy frees up business leaders at every level to pursue the right results in the confidence that they are supported by those above.

People Development

Developing Business Managers who can perform at a high level is in many ways the Group Manager's greatest contribution to the enterprise. Unfortunately, Group Managers don't always recognize people development as their highest priority, preferring to focus on Financial Results that provide faster and more recognizable success. Business Managers who report to them take this implied direction and become reluctant to invest their time and energy in people development. Business Manager development is a long process, and a good deal of effort is required.

Group Managers identify Business Manager candidates early in their careers—ideally, at the Manager of Managers level. They require plans for these candidates that involve coaching, meaningful job rotation, experience in more than one function, and development of appropriate leadership skills. To make it happen, Group Managers champion the succession planning process. Getting personally involved at the Manager of Managers level is required to identify the likely Function Managers. Business Managers recommend their choices for Function Manager but the Group Manager has final approval. So, the Group Manager must acquire deep knowledge of the ability and interest of high-performing Managers of Managers. Developing Function Managers for Business Manager roles is equally important, but this should be considered the minimum requirement.

Effective coaching for Business Managers, particularly when they are new in the role, can make the difference between meeting profit targets and missing them. Instinctively, many Group Managers want to give new Business Managers lots of room to prove themselves. That's fine in the long run, but early on Business

Managers require a significant amount of coaching. As the next chapter will explain, the transition to Business Manager is the hardest to make of all the transitions defined in *The Leadership Pipeline*. Coaching should be done early and often.

Enterprise Leadership

When a CEO meets with her direct reports, that collection of people is called the Policy Committee or the Executive Leadership Team or the Management Board (we'll use "Policy Committee" here). The Policy Committee must have an enterprise focus while doing their work, yet as I've noted, these committee members often prefer a narrower, more self-interested perspective to this enterprise mind-set. An effective Group Manager steps up to the challenge by being a champion of enterprise leadership. Preparing properly for the meetings, supporting the ideas of others, sharing information, staying focused on the big picture, and making an enterprise-based case for her suggestions are basic requirements.

What the Group Manager must deliver

- Portfolio strategy

- New ventures

- Approved business strategy

- Business Manager succession

- Business Manager and Function Manager coaching and development

- Enterprise leadership role model

What the Group Manager enables

- The framework for business strategy

- Coaching for Business Managers and Function Managers

- Development for Managers of Managers

- A succession system for building Business Managers

- Connection with the enterprise strategic framework

Management Results

When it comes to this results category, Group Managers often make the following mistake: trying to manage the businesses rather than trying to manage the Business Managers. Group Managers usually were Business Managers on the way up and were successful in that role. Hanging on to that role is common because Business Manager jobs are full of action and important decisions; many Group Managers say the Business Manager role was much more rewarding. Great care is needed to make sure Group Managers work as Group Managers, and not as Business Managers.

Transparency

Up-to-date information about the state of each business helps Group Managers make the appropriate resource trade-offs. Group Managers should establish the process for information flow. Deciding what information is needed, when it is needed, and what form it should take are defined by the Group Manager. Transparency in reporting helps Group Managers, the Corporate Functions, and the CEO make better decisions.

Delegation

Businesses need to take appropriate risks, manage those risks, and produce results. Group Managers delegate sufficient authority to enable risk-taking and risk management. At the same time, however, Group Managers must implement control mechanisms to keep excessive risk-taking from happening and to be sure that proper risk management is happening. Supporting the CEO's "immune system" (discussed in the previous chapter) and making sure it works helps the Group Manager monitor progress.

Reviews

One element of the control system is the operating review process. Regular operating reviews allow the Group Manager to see the results and hear about progress and obstacles. Candor is critical, and the Group Manager sets the tone and standards for the meetings. Reviews also provide the opportunity for building the team and creating a healthy work environment. Keeping these meetings relevant and constructive so that they don't become perfunctory "dog and pony shows" can be challenging. Establishing the right metrics is one key. Scoreboards are somewhat useful here, but they don't make individual accountability for results clear enough. Business goals and measurements that are unique to the individual and the business are more useful.

What the Group Manager must deliver

- Process for information flow
- Delegation
- Control systems
- Operating reviews
- Metrics for the group
- Open work environment

What the Group Manager enables

- Transparency
- Authority
- Standards for performance
- Appropriate metrics for the businesses

Relationship Results

When Group Managers fail to reach the performance requirements of their levels, it's often because they have given short shrift to a multiplicity of relationships. Many times they do so because building and maintaining these relationships is seen as the primary responsibility of other managers at other levels. In fact, a critical Group Manager responsibility to support enterprise success is assisting in the development and maintenance of these relationships. While the need for effective working relationships with those in layers below is well understood, other relationships may not be as obvious.

For instance, Group Managers should develop *government relationships* on behalf of the enterprise, creating true partnerships when possible. CEOs can't do it all so they rely on Group Managers to share the burden. Corporate Functions also share in this work. Identifying the right people, building constructive and ethical relationships, and conveying the enterprise's commitment to good government make this challenging work.

Customer relationships, too, are a shared responsibility. As with governments, CEOs can't possibly build working relationships with a large number or wide range of key customers. Group Managers must take up some of the slack. Again, customer partnerships are the goal. Like the CEO, Group Managers should not upset the selling process but build relationships that enable joint planning for future business with a long-term focus on mutual benefit.

Group Managers also should forge strong *industry relationships* to obtain information and ideas for developing portfolio strategy. Industry experts, competitors, thought leaders, and associations can provide valuable insight on new directions and confirmation on negative trends. For enterprises with businesses in many industries, the Group Manager should be the enterprise spokesperson in the industries relevant to his businesses. Sharing what he learns with the businesses under him benefits the whole organization.

Alliances and partnerships that have been entered into for business growth or development can be full of difficult relationship problems; Group Managers are often in an excellent position to facilitate these collaborative efforts. Deciding what direction to take, entering new markets, experimentation, sharing intellectual property, and many other actions can lead to disagreements. In many cases, Group Managers can and should be responsible for encouraging the transparency and flexibility that help these partnerships flourish, while eliminating or addressing the disagreements.

Peer relationships are the fifth area where Group Managers need to take responsibility for the enterprise. Working well with colleagues will help make the enterprise successful. Ego, ambition, different agendas, lack of respect, and an unwillingness to compromise are common flaws among Group Managers. It stands to reason that Group Managers have reached their organization level because they are strong personalities; their belief in themselves has been reinforced by their success. Yet when they fail to work well with other individuals or in teams, people notice. Those at lower layers take their cues from this level in how they should work with counterparts in other groups or functions. Group Managers can build silo walls or tear them down by the example they set.

Finally, *relationships with the CEO and Board of Directors* have to be worked at regularly rather than taken for granted. Group Managers have an obligation to their boss to understand what she is trying to accomplish for the enterprise. CEOs must be able to count on the effort and goodwill of their direct reports even if external activities reduce the amount of time they spend together discussing the issues. The board, too, has to trust the Group Managers. It has to believe they will deliver and that the future is being looked after. Since the board represents the shareholders, board members need to know that both short-term and long-term investors will be served properly. Thus, Group Managers need to communicate and demonstrate to both CEOs and board members that they "get" what's important to them and that they're on the same wavelength when it comes to these objectives.

What the Group Manager must deliver

- Government relationships

- Customer partnerships

- Industry relationships

- Partner and alliance relationships

- Peer relationships

- Upward relationships

- Subordinate relationships

What the Group Manager enables

- Receptive customers

- A climate of collaboration

- Benefits from external relationships

- Good citizenship

- Industry analyses and trends

Example

Derek had been Chief Executive of Snelling Company, a regional consumer goods manufacturer with a strong history of growth. Snelling was organized as one business with a big sales force but very small support staff. When Snelling was acquired by Bravo Enterprises, Derek was told they wanted him to stay on and run his business. After much discussion with the Bravo CEO, Derek agreed to stay.

Two months later Derek was asked to run his business plus two others in his part of the world, and that his title would be Executive Vice President, Middle East Region. He was now a Group Manager responsible for three businesses, a totally new role for him. After meeting with the senior teams in each of his new businesses, he reflected on what he had learned:

- Both new business teams were unhappy about being acquired, just as his own team was. They resented the loss of autonomy and didn't like Bravo, well known to them from head-to-head competition.

- They resented him because he had no real standing at Bravo and would probably just meddle in their business, as they knew him by reputation as a hands-on Business Manager.

- None of the business teams including his own wanted to work with Bravo Corporate Staff, which everyone viewed as unnecessary overhead.

These were new problems for Derek, and he wasn't sure how to address them.

After attending the Bravo CEO's monthly meeting, Derek asked one of his peers, the EVP for Latin America, how he had organized his region. The peer suggested that he get Margret, the VP for Organization Development, to help work up a plan, just as she had done for him. Part of that plan had been to clearly define the results expected for him, and the results expected for the Business Managers, so that the roles would be clear. Derek invited Margret to meet him at his office in Dubai to do something similar for him.

Margret spent a day working with Derek on defining his role as Region Manager and the Business Manager roles that *reported to him. She used the performance standards Bravo had adopted to explain the differences between Business Manager results and Group Manager results. After talking through the roles, it became clear to Derek that he had to replace himself in the former Snelling business, so he called his Head of Sales and asked him to take the job. Next he asked his three Business Managers to join him the following day to discuss roles and responsibilities and working arrangements.*

With Margret facilitating the discussion, Derek and his new team spent most of the day discussing how to make the Middle East Region successful and how to make each of their businesses successful as well as themselves. Everyone had much to learn about Bravo Enterprises, Derek's role, and their own roles in this new situation.

The team meeting was so candid and productive that it spilled over to the next day. Everyone was pleased to hear Margret's examples of how experts in Corporate Staff had helped other regions and businesses. The Business Managers were also grateful for the opportunity to discuss their roles with their new boss. It became crystal clear that Derek had to be their champion at Bravo. They were used to making their own capital decisions at their previous companies but now had to live with Bravo's processes. Corporate help on marketing promotions, customer information, logistics planning, and information technology were also of interest. Derek realized that he needed corporate cooperation and support to be successful. The meeting concluded with agreements on what the Business Managers would "own," what reporting to Derek would be like, a small plan for getting to know firsthand what the Corporate Staff could contribute, and what Derek would do to help the region grow and gain stature in the Middle East and with Bravo.

During the following week, Derek met with his boss, the CEO of Bravo, to present the definition of his new region executive position and show that it could work to everyone's benefit. The CEO gave him a clear picture of his expectations for an Executive Vice President. Taking ownership for Bravo's success, working collaboratively with the senior team, and delivering on the financials were at the top of the list. The CEO said he would revise the Bravo Region Manager Performance Standards, as on the basis of the conversation some new requirements were needed, particularly on the working relationships.

Group Manager Performance Standards

Table 3.1 contains the revised Region Manager standards at Bravo ("Co. B."). The original standards had been developed to help Bravo pursue its goal of global leadership in their industry. Snelling and others were acquired as part of that goal. While Region Managers were asked to focus upward and outward, there wasn't enough emphasis on looking downward to make the individual businesses and their leaders successful. The additions in *italics* in the table were made to reflect the importance of Region Managers (Group Managers) in enabling that success.

This company put the required work values in the second column to emphasize that working at the right layer was expected of all employees, including those of the acquired companies. Being acquired changed the layer for many senior people.

I have shared this example because it illustrates how logical it is for Group Managers to connect the business to the enterprise and the enterprise to the business. It is also clear that relationships are complicated and working on the things that really matter is the best way to build them.

The meeting with Derek and his team happened and spilled into a second day as described. No one could recall ever spending that much time on getting roles and working relationships properly

Table 3.1 Executive Vice President, Region (Group Manager)

Performance Dimensions	Required Work Values	Full Performance
Business Results		
• Development of global capability	• Global business success. • World-class thinking at world-class levels.	• Business/Function results enable [Co. B.] to deliver targeted shareholder value. • Centers of Excellence are world class.
• Major Projects	• No turf.	• Growth rate exceeds industry, year after year. • High level projects identified and delivered.
• Management Committee Effectiveness	• Shareholder value. • Social Responsibility.	• Global brands and potential global brands are nurtured and protected.
• Centers of Excellence		
• Balanced Global Network	• An owner's view of results.	• Track record of delivering/exceeding profit and growth targets, consistently over five years.
• Operating Methods	• Group market share growth.	• Proactively connected and leveraged the Businesses to get additional results when [Co. B.] needs dictate.
• Brands	• Group business success.	• Championed acquisitions that improve share earnings/image and rapidly assimilated into [Co. B.] community.
• Strategic Imperatives		
• Group Profit		
• Group Growth		• Supply chain effectiveness set global standard.
• New Ventures		

(Continued)

Table 3.1 (*Continued*)

Performance Dimensions	Required Work Values	Full Performance
Leadership Results • [Co. B.] Leadership • Corporate Strategy and Group Strategy Development • Motivated Team • Right People In the Right Place • Coaching and Development	• Management Committee Champion. • World-class talent. • Staffing to strategy. • *Success of Business Managers.*	• Role model for Management Committee membership. • Directly impacts the development of [Co. B.] enterprise strategy. • Group's strategy understood throughout. • Role model for guiding principles. • Recruits/Coaches for world-class performance. • Effective [Co. B.] spokesperson internally and externally. • Net source of energy to the Group. • *Connected the businesses to the Enterprise.* • *Built Business Leader succession.* • *Put the right Business Managers in place and got the wrong ones out.* • *Group's capability improved every year.* • *Group programs demonstrably enhanced [Co. B.]'s business capability.*
Management Results • Delegation • Reallocation • Appropriate Metrics • Risk Analysis and Management • Priorities/Resources Alignment • Operations Review And Follow-Up • Plan Reviews • Alignment Of Markets With Company Strategy	• Effective oversight. • Transparency. • Flawless execution. • World-class governance. • *Getting results through Business Managers.*	• Clearly defined and measured delegation and control system in place. • Strategic uncertainties closely monitored. • Right results at right time. • Business information flows quickly and accurately. • Metrics in place that enable early warning. • Transaction costs reduced each year. • No surprises. • Projects flawlessly executed. • *Regular operating reviews of business management results held in all markets.* • *Resources allocated and reallocated to assure Business and Enterprise results are achieved.*

Relationship Results
- Government Relations (for Group, with shareholder view)
- Market-Level Connection
- Management Committee
- External Board
- Strategic Alliances

- Representing [Co. B.] externally.
- Statesmanship.
- Executive teamwork.
- Free flow of information internally.

- Focused on the common good at [Co. B.].
- Open and candid with External Board and its members.
- Key external partners willingly support [Co. B.].
- Peers kept fully informed.
- End Market relationships enable open, frequent dialogue in both directions.
- Advice given to Chairman, Managing Director, fellow Directors was researched and reflected a group perspective.
- Built government partnerships for Group and shareholder benefit.
- *Proactively developed sound working relationships with senior government officials in the Region.*
- *Actively supported Functional strategy.*

Innovation Results
- Culture of (value-added innovation and change) leveraging multi-national/cross border insights

- Innovation that leverages business results.
- Wide diversity of sources for information and ideas.
- Innovation across the business—all levels, all functions.
- Speedy application of good ideas.

- Created an environment throughout the organization which encouraged challenge, innovation and change.
- Leveraged understanding of customers, consumers, suppliers, internal and external stakeholders, to inform business decisions.
- Results indicate use of new ideas.
- *Made the space and the time to challenge, reflect upon and revisit assumptions about the business model, practices and processes.*

defined. An agreement was reached to review the roles and relationships every six months.

Results We Don't Want from Group Managers

Transitioning to the Group Manager layer has many traps and pitfalls. It's easy to get it wrong. Spelling out results Group Managers should *not* produce helps to clarify the role and keeps them from interfering with the work of the Business Managers.

Business strategy. It is easy for Group Managers to take over the strategy development process for the businesses in their portfolio. They got promoted to Group Manager because they were effective at developing and executing business strategy. Direct reports, particularly the ones who are new at managing a business, are likely to defer to them. Group Managers critique business strategy, ask the right questions, challenge the assumptions, and press for alternatives, but they don't develop the answers or the strategy. Business Managers must learn to think strategically and develop sound business strategies on their own.

Competition with Business Managers. Instilling confidence and building skills in Business Managers helps get the right results for the businesses and for the enterprise. No matter how tempting it is or how easy it would be, Group Managers must not show off their superiority or pick fights with the Business Managers. A trust-based relationship with appropriate coaching is the best approach. Holding the Business Manager accountable for delivering results can be done without conveying superiority. Broken relationships between these two layers can disconnect the business from the enterprise.

Silos. A strong focus on the success of the group can lead to forgetting about or ignoring other groups and the Corporate Staff. When the groups are in different industries or different regions, it is particularly easy to forget about everyone else. When that happens, the enterprise is weakened, key relationships don't get built, and information doesn't flow. Business opportunities may get lost. The CEO's purpose gets subverted (usually this isn't the intention), so he gets unhappy and career-threatening conversations may result. This is a common scenario, and it doesn't get fixed through staff meetings. Setting aside time for peers and peer organizations can head off a lot of trouble and produce some useful results.

CEO Succession Candidates

Finally, I would be remiss in our discussion of Group Manager requirements if I failed to mention the succession issue. Choosing the next CEO internally has about a ten times greater probability of success than hiring an outside candidate. Group Managers and the Chief Financial Officer are the most likely contenders. Accepting responsibility for enterprise success, building peer and key external relationships, representing the enterprise to direct reports and partners of all kinds, and developing portfolio strategy are all crucial preparation for CEO candidates. Therefore, Group Managers must master these skills, not only so they can perform their job at a high level but so that if they are named CEO, they can hit the ground running.

Moving an internal candidate up is the best choice. If Group Managers are struggling with some or all of these requirements, however, the CEO may well conclude that new talent should be added. If an external candidate has to be added, it is better to do so at the Group Manager layer than to recruit someone for the CEO position who lacks any internal development. Time is needed to learn the company and build relationships before ascending to the top. With all its pressures and visibility, the CEO layer is an extremely difficult place to enter a new company.

4

Business Managers

Short-Term and Long-Term Profit

This is a high-profile, much sought-after leadership position, but despite its visibility within organizations, the results for this level are often poorly defined. In fact, this is a level that receives a great deal of attention but insufficient definition. Consequently, Business Managers may appear to be doing a good job because they shine in one spotlighted area, but unbeknownst to the organization, they are failing to deliver the total spectrum of results.

Let's start out by providing a proper definition of this role, one that is often lacking in companies. First and foremost, be aware that Business Manager positions have dramatic impact on both the incumbent and the enterprise. Incumbents tend to fall in love with their jobs. Many have told me that having direct control of the critical pieces of a business is stimulating and empowering. Many corporations recognize the importance of this leadership position and invest heavily in development programs and career tracks to get people ready to run businesses. Given that the performance of incumbents is reflected in the enterprise share price, companies remove poor performers more quickly than they do managers at any other layer. Failure rates are second only to Enterprise CEOs. Generally, the emphasis is on profit and the financials. It should be on building a profit-making machine—an organization that delivers under any conditions. As we'll see, performance is hampered when too much focus is on the "score" and not enough focus is on learning to play the game with increasing skill.

To avoid confusion, let me clarify how I'm defining a true Business Manager. Quite simply, this is someone with account-ability for profit and direct decision-making authority for both cost and revenue. Managing the trade-offs between these two require-ments is especially critical; so, having only one or the other responsibility disqualifies an individual from being a Business Manager, at least in terms of the Performance Pipeline. People running product lines are often called Business Managers, but they don't control the cost or sales, so that isn't enough; they are really Function Managers. People running sales organizations are some-times called Business Managers, but they too aren't fully responsible for the bottom line even though they may be measured on it if they don't manage product cost.

True Business Managers also have accountability for several functions, for example, Development or Engineering, Production or Manufacturing, Sales and Marketing, Finance and Human Resources. If the enterprise has only one complete business, the CEO is the de facto Business Manager. When there is more than one business and the Business Managers report to the Enterprise CEO, they have some accountability for Group Manager results. Country Managers in multinational companies often have true Business Manager accountability when they have several functions reporting to them and are responsible for a P&L. Given these various titles, the best way to identify true Business Managers is by making sure they possess cost and revenue accountability. This chapter focuses on things to be done to ensure that profit is deliv-ered now and in the future.

Critical Requirements for Building a Profit-Making Machine

In the previous section I noted that Business Managers are respon-sible for building a profit-making machine. This is significantly different from being responsible for hitting profit targets; Business

Managers who confine themselves to hitting these targets usually hurt their organizations. Ongoing profit requires a Business Manager who can help the organization deliver consistently rather than one who can generate significant profit based on his heroic effort.

Successful Business Managers I have worked with put four key ingredients in place:

1. A value proposition that customers want

2. Strategic alignment

3. Strong working relationships

4. A steady business rhythm

When Business Managers struggle to execute a business strategy, they usually fail. These four ingredients establish direction and make execution possible.

A Value Proposition That Customers Want

Finding the right combination of product offering, price, quality, service, delivery, and the like is the purpose of much strategic thinking and planning by Business Managers. The fit with the group's portfolio strategy and the enterprise strategic framework is essential. The resulting "value proposition" defines the business's purpose. Good Business Managers work at defining a purpose that positions the business for competitive advantage. The value proposition becomes a guiding force for all other leaders and employees. It helps them focus on the right work with the right standard. It makes priority-setting much easier. Most of all, it cuts through the clutter found in most business strategy documents.

Given the rapid rate of change and the high degree of uncertainty that exists in today's environment, many businesses are finding that their current value proposition doesn't work anymore. Customers are not responding the way they used to when times were better. Business Managers must define and implement a value proposition customers want. In many ways, this is the most important result that a Business Manager can deliver.

Example—New Value Proposition Needed

A few years ago, De Beers held over 90 percent market share in uncut diamonds. Despite this dominant position, growth projections for its Diamond Trading Company were relatively flat at a time when other luxury goods were experiencing rapid growth. Sales of designer handbags and shoes, luxury vacations, and top-of-the-line watches were all growing faster than sales of diamond jewelry. The luxury goods market was hot, but not for diamond jewelry. After extensive market research and analysis of stakeholder issues and preferences, the company determined that it had to change. De Beers' mining businesses also had challenges due to rising costs. Return on investment associated with mining costs was falling. The Diamond Trading Company needed major overhaul to get acceptable returns. Raising prices in a flat market or simple cost-cutting would not be enough. The company needed to drive volume and cash in on the hot luxury goods market.

On the basis of sound strategic thinking, De Beers' Business Managers created a new and more relevant value proposition. They decided to work toward becoming the "supplier of choice." In effect they changed from "you have to come to us" to "you want to come to us." Selling practices had to be changed to fit the new value proposition. Rather than requiring customers (called siteholders) to buy a box of assorted diamonds (take it or leave it), they encouraged siteholders to purchase matching stones for jewelry designs that had more than one diamond. Major advertising spending that promoted diamond jewelry with multiple stones (the three-diamond ring) was undertaken. Selling to pure resellers was reduced, and more emphasis was placed on selling to jewelry manufacturers. Perhaps the biggest change was giving up their near monopoly position in uncut diamonds, gaining an important degree of freedom from regulatory constraints. They purposely lowered their market share to less than 50 percent. New market entrants had pushed them in that direction, but the Diamond Trading Company did it on its own terms. The point is that the Business Managers pursued the bold but necessary change and invested in the supporting elements to begin delivering a new, more market-relevant value proposition. Sales and profit grew by double digits for the next several years.

Strategic Alignment

Strategic alignment (Figure 4.1) is the overarching result that Business Managers must produce. All the elements listed in Figure 4.1 require time and attention individually and concerted effort collectively. While creating a new and relevant value proposition may be the most important result for Business Managers today, defining the business strategy remains their primary task. Delivering that strategy by getting all the right elements in place and functioning in rhythm is crucial if that result is to be achieved. The value proposition won't give a business a competitive advantage if that value proposition can't be delivered profitably and predictably because of alignment problems.

Alignment is achieved by being clear about the work required, making sure all the necessary work is assigned, and having people with the capability to do that work. Business Managers "walk the perimeter" of this alignment triangle to make sure all the elements are in place and that they are appropriate for achieving a sustainable competitive advantage.

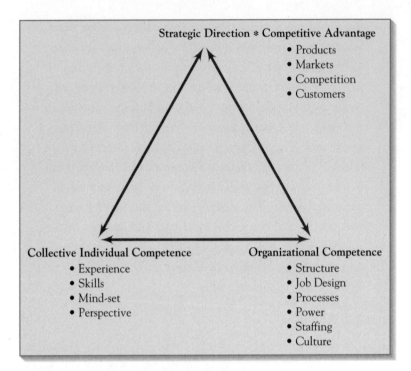

Figure 4.1 Strategic Alignment

Note: All three sides of this triangle must be in alignment for a business to sustain a competitive advantage. When any important change is made in one element, work must be done to bring other elements into complete alignment.

Example

Lee was in his first Country Business Manager position and struggling with a strong cyclical economy that was playing havoc with the business's financials. Lee had taken over eight months earlier in the midst of a severe market downturn. His predecessor had grown the business rapidly during the last boom, and the business had become bloated with employees and half-completed large-scale projects. Lee's strategy had been to cut back drastically on expenses while encouraging Marketing to find some niches to exploit during the downturn. Employees had been let go and projects cut back. Nonetheless, profitability had dropped to unacceptable levels.

As the economy stabilized and began growing, though, the business failed to respond. Marketing had introduced two successful programs in the last year, and even those were faltering.

To create strategic alignment, Lee began by identifying all the key challenges the business faced, including these:

- *Customers were defecting, but the source of their dissatisfaction was ambiguous. It could be service problems, or it could be new programs that were now available from other competitors. No one was sure why customers were leaving.*

- *The Marketing team was weak. While many had been with the business a long time and were hardworking and dedicated, their focus tended to be narrow and insular. Long-standing interpersonal conflicts had been left unresolved by a series of managers. Lee had seen his Marketing Head's direct reports pursue individual and contradictory agendas at times.*

- *Operations had been slow to respond on previous customer programs, and their leadership was second-rate. The Operations Manager complained that the newest service programs had been introduced before staffing and service guidelines had been fully defined and established.*

- *Finance had a history of poor collaboration with the rest of the organization. Accurate financial data was always slow in coming. Lee had received a number of complaints from his peers that the CFO was unresponsive to requests to participate in company-wide finance initiatives including improving the budget process.*

Lee had to address all of these challenges, but he had to do so in a way that fit it all together. He needed to get everyone and everything focused on the same target to produce sustainable results. An integrated solution was needed, including hiring a new Marketing Head who could find out what customers wanted and build a better Marketing team, insisting on teamwork from his direct reports, pushing for better financial data, and developing a better business strategy and value proposition. Cost-cutting and revenue enhancement would not lead to sustained business success without customer information, teamwork, and strategy.

In some situations, Business Managers address all the challenges the business faces, but they do so in segregated or disconnected ways. For this reason, their performance suffers because the business doesn't improve sufficiently.

Achieving alignment is difficult, and maintaining it is equally difficult. Effective Business Managers overcome this difficulty by examining all the challenges continuously, making sure they're the right ones to be examining, and ensuring that all actions regarding these issues are coordinated and focused on one target.

Alignment cannot be achieved if the business doesn't have the right people for the required work. That corner of the alignment triangle always deserves substantial attention when the Business Manager "walks the perimeter." There can't be alignment if the leadership team isn't strong enough to carry it down to the lowest levels of the business. Everyone must have a mind-set of "I am here to deliver customer value."

Finally, when dealing with strategic alignment, Business Managers must employ the approach I have been referring to,

"Walking the perimeter." This must be done regularly and must involve analysis, dialogue, firsthand observation, testing, and coaching. Most of the individual elements are the responsibility of someone else. Their appropriateness and connection are the Business Manager's overarching contribution.

Strong Working Relationships

When it comes to results, many Business Managers might not put relationship-building at the top of their lists. It seems like too "soft" a goal for someone at their level. Yet relationships "lubricate" the work, getting people to move faster and more efficiently as they go about their tasks. Customers, too, are more receptive when relationships are positive. Employees are less cynical, and suppliers are more supportive when relationships are strong. While Business Managers can't dictate that everyone must get along, they can take responsibility for relationships by setting the tone for positive collaboration. This doesn't mean they should give talks and send e-mails encouraging a cooperative attitude. Rather, they should model the behavior they want others to adopt.

As teachers are fond of telling their students, this isn't a popularity contest. Business Managers don't have to be liked by everyone; nor, for that matter, do they have to like all the people they work with. One Business Manager told me that his standard was quite simple. He said, "If you and I work together today, we should want to work together again tomorrow, no matter how hard we had to work, how long we had to work, how difficult the work was, or how difficult the situation was." Building trust through honest effort, a constructive attitude, being fair, finishing, showing concern, and communicating honestly are the actions this statement encourages.

While Business Managers need to cultivate a variety of relationships, two are the most critical—and often the most problematic. First, they must work well with all direct reports. This may seem a given, but in fact, many Business Managers favor one or two direct reports over all the others. Typically, Business Managers have come up through one function and quite naturally understand its value. Making time for its leader comes easily. Other functional heads may not be able to get appropriate time and attention because the Business Manager doesn't know what the function can really do or doesn't value some functions based on negative experiences in the past. Unless all functions are valued and their leaders treated with the same respect, quality and team-work will suffer. The performance of the disrespected function will probably be minimally acceptable. Silos will inevitably form as a means of self-defense. The real crime here is that the best people leave.

The second critical relationship is with Group Managers, who help Business Managers focus on the enterprise. Because Business Managers have essentially a self-contained organization—several functions, their own strategy and customers, and their own operating plan and budget—they frequently ignore the enterprise or feel little accountability for the enterprise's success. Corporate Staff Functions are viewed as problems to be avoided. More than one Business Manager has complained, "I have a business to run!" when asked to participate in an enterprise initiative. This is a major mistake that will detract from performance. Their businesses can't be successful for long if the enterprise isn't successful.

A Steady Business Rhythm

Great businesses have a rhythm, a way of working that is relatively smooth and well-paced. Product ideas get converted into product designs. Designs are manufactured. Customer engagement is turned into a sale of those products, which produces cash. Cash is invested for more products or new products. People are able to do their jobs because they know what is expected and know when their work fits. Everyone is properly prepared and trained. Effective communication and teamwork are seen and heard everywhere.

You can literally feel that rhythm when you engage with the business. An energy exists that is palpable—you can walk the office hallways, enter a meeting, or observe a team at work, and you sense the excitement and commitment. Similarly, you can feel it when businesses lack rhythm. Disagreements, misunderstandings, missing or inferior work, and a lack of information create a disconnectedness to the work, a lack of coordination and smooth functioning. While walking the perimeter to see if all the right elements are in place, the Business Manager has to also observe the flow of work and hear the tone when individuals and organizations are working together.

A steady business rhythm is built on individuals and organizations trusting each other to do the right thing and having confidence in each other's ability to perform. As a result, work can flow smoothly because there is little or no conflict between the individuals involved or reluctance to respond to requests. Resources have to be available when needed so that work can get done without waiting. Everyone has to be clear about the plans and priorities. Stress that comes from overwork, conflicting priorities, and a lack of support from the manager must be addressed. Cynics, poor performers, selfish people, and uncooperative people have to be changed or weeded out. Perfection is not required, but problem situations, problem people, and problem processes have to be addressed. Business Managers need to have a sense of where the work flow problems come from so they can fix them at the source.

Either Business Managers get the rhythm going or they don't. In uncertain times, markets stop and go, customers change their requirements, and suppliers tumble; a rhythmic approach provides reassurance and stability and keeps managers sane.

Summary of Critical Results

Again, I'm providing a summary that breaks down the results for this level into deliverables and enabling results. Be aware that I've restated the four results categories just discussed plus added results that support the four critical results. The enabling results listed are things needed at lower levels to help those levels succeed. These are particularly important for Business Managers, since they make the business work better.

What the Business Manager must deliver

- Market-relevant value propositions
- Strategic analysis
- Complete alignment
- Integrated functions
- Effective working relationships up and down
- Equal value for all functions
- Steady business rhythm
- Trust and confidence

What the Business Manager enables

- A focus on value proposition—ensures that every employee knows what the endgame is
- Strategic context—gives every employee the same picture
- Rhythm for the business—makes it easier to get the job done for everyone
- Equal treatment for all functions—keeps support staff, in particular, from feeling like second-class citizens
- Role model for relationships—sets the tone for how to work together

- Integrated functional work—gets everyone pulling in the same direction

The Whole Job and the Measurements

Business Managers have a broad range of results to deliver beyond those already discussed. Table 4.1 lays out the whole job as performance standards developed by Company E. Based in the Midwest portion of the United States, Company E makes and sells chemical compounds that are used for a variety of commercial applications in hospitality, food, health care industries, and in the home. The company asked for a performance pipeline to help with their enterprise-wide drive for profitable growth, including growth in other countries.

While putting together their performance pipeline, we discovered that some Business Managers valued growth, but it wasn't their first priority. We decided that more emphasis had to be placed on measuring growth so that Business Managers would recognize the importance of this type of result. To that end, a specific results category called "Growth" was established, which highlighted the subject and defined some key growth-based results. The company also defined growth strategies for the business that took into consideration the growth of other businesses. Examining and pursuing new markets as well as new applications for existing products was another important measure.

Beyond the growth category, growth-related items such as acquisitions and "unlocking the organization's energy" (securing greater commitment, focus, and creativity) became part of Business Managers' performance standards. Company E also emphasized productivity and cost management as a result to balance the normal desire to pursue growth at the expense of profit.

Finally, the company held Business Managers accountable for talent—growing and selecting the right leaders was a major

Table 4.1 Chemical/Commercial Products Company, Business Manager

Shift in Work Values
- From results through function to results through comprehensive business management
- From state-of-the-art results to business success
- From functional excellence to customer value
- From planning for functional results to creating long-term strategic plans

Results	Full Performance	Exceptional Performance	Skills, Knowledge, and Experience
Business/Functional Results • Sales, OI, SG&A • Competitive analysis • Value proposition • Resource strategy • Economic environment • Acquisition decisions	• Planned short-term business results are delivered without compromising long-term growth • Competitive advantage is sustainable • Value proposition meets and anticipates customer needs and [Co. E's] needs • Economic, political, competitive, market and industry knowledge is evident in strategy and decision making • Acquisitions are evaluated holistically and from a strategic mindset	• Profit grows faster than revenue • Competitive advantage is achieved through innovation • Value proposition leads the industry • Acquisitions are seamlessly integrated	• Understanding of financial impact of decisions • Business planning; deep knowledge of the contribution of each function • Must know where to go for data and how to interpret business implications • Ability to think tactically and strategically • Able to think in terms of profitability and sustainability rather than functional capability • Must know how to read and interpret market data and competitive response

Management
- Operational planning
- Organizational structure
- Manage the business
- Focus
- Strategic problem solving
- Drive strategy
- Safety

- Organizational energy is directed toward achieving business results
- Functional activity fully integrated and aligned including Operations, RD&E and support functions, through the operational plan
- Immune system in place and fully functioning
- Reviews (project reviews, MPR, plan reviews) are conducted to drive decisions rather than share information
- Business strategy is executed at optimal cost
- Safety strategy supports achieving business results

- Organizational energy is superior to peers' and competitors'
- Breakthrough results are achieved through industry leading strategies
- Business units fully integrated and aligned through platform delivery
- Business practices emulated by competition

- Ability to make hard decisions and courage to stay the course
- Contingency planning
- Ability to architect an organization to support strategy
- Ability to select and assess functional leaders based on business strategy
- Ability to anticipate and avoid problems
- Ability to problem solve at the root cause level
- Multi-functional experience

Leadership
- Personal leadership
- Team strength
- Enable functional leadership
- Performance culture
- Influence
- Strategic vision
- Company capability
- Cross-selling culture

- Personally connected to associates at all levels
- Team strength is matched to strategic requirements
- "A" performance is delivered by every team member
- Organizational champion for developing a diverse talent pipeline
- Use of power is balanced and appropriate to both building strong functional leaders and take business risks
- Business strategy delivers competitive advantage, is understood and accepted by the business and the Company
- Results show tangible evidence of cross-division support

- Role model for embodiment of corporate values and directives
- Team performs with or without involvement of General Manager
- Viewed as a premier employer by diverse talent inside and outside of organization
- Sought out by various parts of organization for coaching and strategic thinking
- Strategy emulated by competition
- Opportunities for partnering cross-divisionally or internationally are actively leveraged

- High integrity
- Respectful of others
- Willingness to rely on and have confidence in functional leaders to achieve results
- Knowing how to build alliances in order to get things done
- Ability to create a future that people want to be a part of
- Articulate communicator and effective listener

(Continued)

Table 4.1 (Continued)

Results	Full Performance	Exceptional Performance	Skills, Knowledge, and Experience
Relationships • Key customer relationships • Subordinate and senior executive relationships • Peer relationships • Company spokesperson • Community relations • Political relationships	• Senior-level partnerships established with customers • Strong working relationships with each team member and each senior executive • Climate supports relationship building at all levels and throughout organization • Advance [Co. E] in the industry and analyst community by acting as persuasive Company spokesperson as appropriate • [Co. E] representative in community through participation on boards and community initiatives	• Senior level partnerships with customers are leveraged for [Co. E's] growth • Deliberately eliminates boundaries between business and between business and corporate functions • Influence and insight sought by community and industry leaders for advancement of initiatives	• Appreciate relationships for the sake of relationships • Ability to make friends with everyone • Ability to understand what is driving other people • Ability to read powerful people and complex situations • Comfortable in a leadership role • Well read in current events • Understands the greater good
Growth • Growth strategy • New markets • New applications • Innovation • New products and services	• Growth strategy results in profitable growth within own business as well as other [Co. E] businesses • Business processes are continually improved and/or exploit growth opportunities and/or lower cost • Investments are leveraged to create new markets and new applications • Acquisitions are completed based on world-class analysis and meet performance expectations	• [Co. E] is embedded in customer strategy • Individual accountability among team is expanded to increase individual contribution • Customers invest in new products and applications	• Intellectual curiosity • Market intelligence • Ability to think broadly and long term • Ability and willingness to exploit the market • Open-minded and tolerant of difference • Willingness to take risks and to learn from mistakes • Willingness to experiment and try new things

requirement. It wanted to be sure that growth was properly managed and that sufficient numbers would be ready to fill new positions. Company E chose to identify the skills, knowledge, and experience required for success at this layer, especially because they wanted to be sure that staffing decisions, development plans, and coaching would be focused on enabling the growth agenda.

As you can see, more results requirements exist than the primary four that I outlined earlier in the chapter. I've gone into detail here so that you can get a sense of the entire results "gestalt" for the Business Manager layer. Table 4.1 provides specific definition of results that Business Managers must deliver.

Pay special attention to the "Exceptional Performance" column, since this was critical to Company E when it created its pipeline. Ensuring true understanding of the difference between full performance and exceptional performance created a new target for high-achievers. It also kept full-performers who slightly exceeded their goals from feeling they were exceptional and deserved exceptional rewards.

This company had a strong interest in leadership development, so much time and effort went into producing the fourth column, "Skills, Knowledge, and Experience." Developing on the job was a big part of the company's development approach, so it wanted a comprehensive list for use by the boss, HR, and outside coaches. Complete mastery of the list was not its expectation. Rather, it wanted to know what avenues to pursue when development was needed or desired, as in becoming a better leader or building better relationships.

Business Managers have complicated jobs, and a wide variety of skills and abilities are needed. Successful Business Managers bring many key abilities to the job, but many more are developed on the job. Column four is highly recommended for every set of performance standards so that incumbents can self-assess and pursue development on their own. Specific guidance for helpers is also of real value.

Inappropriate Results for Business Managers

The main way that Business Managers miss the mark on results involves doing too much. Because they have much to deliver that is unique to their role, they should have little time left for doing things others should do (or no one should do). Business Managers must stay focused on the four critical requirements, which no one else should produce, while giving the Function Managers room to lead their functions. As I noted earlier, failure to deliver the needed results invites the Group Manager to run the business and essentially means that three layers are now failing to deliver expected results.

Because it's so easy for Business Managers to overstep their roles or fail to recognize what responsibilities are mission-critical, consider the following results we *don't* want Business Managers to produce:

All decisions. In smaller businesses, the Business Manager frequently becomes a hub through which all decisions pass. It happens because the Business Manager wants it to happen (sometimes subconsciously). In these cases, Business Managers end up chained to their desks. Long days of working on the wrong things, failure to develop decision-making skills in the Function Managers, and insufficient effort on defining the future are the consequences. If the Business Manager doesn't trust her people to make decisions, or if her people choose to delegate all decisions to her, she should recruit some more capable people for her team as quickly as possible.

Isolation. The need for thinking time, external obligations, customer visits, and time with the Group Manager add up to significant time away from the business and its people. As a result, many people grouse that "he doesn't care about us." Cynicism can also spread in a business where the Business Manager isn't visible enough. Keeping all employees positive and motivated to deliver the value proposition is necessary, and Business Managers can't do this if they're not around. External activities have to be balanced with the internal requirements.

Functional leadership. I've cautioned against this before, but it bears repeating: Business Managers who have been high-performing Function Managers can easily revert to their former role after being promoted to Business Manager. When they revert, they limit the results they can deliver as well as the results the Function Manager is supposed to deliver. Business Managers should be making sure that Function Managers deliver appropriate results and learn to lead their function. Business Managers should also make sure everyone works at the right level.

Corporate animosity. When Business Managers thumb their nose at corporate initiatives or simply ignore them, it produces animosity from the top. There isn't any upside to this result. Business Managers hurt their reputation, and they will be forced to comply with corporate mandates eventually. While Business Managers have every right to voice their disagreement over the value or purpose of the corporate initiative, they should talk with Group or Corporate Function Managers rather than be rebellious or become passive-aggressive. After making their case to the appropriate party, Business Managers must live with the outcome of the discussion. There is a bigger picture, and Business Managers have to see it.

5

Function Managers
Competitive Advantage

When people are promoted to Function Manager, they are excited to be at the top of their profession in a business. They report to a Business Manager and are part of a business team, and their peers run different functions. When only one business exists, they report to the CEO, and some double as Corporate Function Managers. Since their boss in either of these situations is probably not a product of their function, they don't get much technical guidance; they do receive business guidance that they translate into functional requirements. In turn, they provide technical guidance to the Business Manager, especially when she hasn't worked in the function. Facilitating business decision making with sound functional information is an important part of the role.

The primary purpose of Function Managers is to give their business a competitive advantage by delivering functional results that are better than the competition's. The business achieves its goals and improves its competitive position through the ability of the Function Manager to deliver. Unfortunately, Function Managers misinterpret their role frequently and hurt the business. This negative outcome can be prevented by building the right performance expectations. I'll discuss how to do so as well as how to increase the odds that Function Managers deliver the results they're supposed to deliver.

Who Are the Function Managers?

Let's define our terms, since some confusion exists about this managerial level because of various business trends and other developments. At first glance, this level might seem easy to define—each major work discipline in a business is a function: Engineering, Manufacturing, Marketing, Human Resources, and so on. Consider, though, where confusion can arise. Information Technology (IT) used to be put under Finance in many companies but is now quite critical and is usually treated as a separate function. Strategic Planning and Supply Chain, also relatively recent arrivals in terms of existence and importance, are also considered functions now. In addition, debate can exist whether to split Marketing and Sales into two functions. If both of these Function Managers report to the Business Manager and sit on the business team, then both can be considered to be functions. Quality Control and Safety, too, are frequently split out for special emphasis. If a Business Manager chooses to have them (either or both) report to him directly, they can be considered functions, although they would normally be part of the Manufacturing or Operations function. Role definition is often too narrow.

Example—A Narrowly Focused Function Manager

When Function Managers fail to perform at a level that's required, it's often because of their deceptively successful performance. In other words, they excel at leading the function in one area, and this performance obscures their deficits in other key results areas—obscures them temporarily, that is, until negative consequences eventually emerge.

BRC, a business that makes coloring additives for a variety of applications, brought in Chris as Vice President of Marketing. The enterprise comprised six businesses, and BRC was the smallest. In general, the Marketing function was weak across the enterprise. BRC had grown fast over its first few years because of one great application, but its growth stalled. New customers and new applications were needed. To help fix the problem, the company began a search for a VP of Marketing and found Chris, who seemed like an ideal hire. Previously, she had been the Marketing Function Manager in two businesses about the same size as BRC, though they were part of much smaller enterprises.

Chris inherited a number of challenges, including a small staff of widely varying abilities, a lack of expertise in marketing work, and an absence of a defined role and space for the Marketing function on the business team. In terms of this last challenge, Chris's predecessor was an "order taker" and hadn't carved out much time for the function at business team meetings or gained much respect from peers. Fortunately for Chris, her reputation preceded her, and her peers and the Marketing team greeted her enthusiastically.

Chris's Functional Results were strong for the first year and even stronger for the second. Excellent strategic analysis and market planning helped her identify and open new markets. She coached her team, and they became more skillful at market and customer analysis, customer engagement, and selling. She added a talented market-development person who found more product capability through a partnership with his former company. Because of her acumen, Chris helped the company achieve double-digit sales growth in her first two years.

Her success was obvious, but her record was not without blemish. Some of her peers began to complain about her to the Business Manager: Chris didn't involve them in her thinking and planning; Operations was racing to keep up, but quality was slipping; Finance didn't feel that it had time for credit checks on new customers; Human Resources was concerned that two of Chris's Marketing stars had fared poorly in interviews for leadership positions in the other *businesses; customers began complaining about errors on their bills and declining product quality. By the middle of the third year, Chris had become alienated from her peers, and profit growth was half the rate of the sales growth. The Business Manager felt he had to step in and get help for Chris. She was now isolated from her peers.*

This was not all Chris's fault. If a performance pipeline had been in place, she and her boss would have been clear about the range of results she needed to produce, and the pipeline's specificity would have ensured appropriate accountability. As skilled as Chris was at building sales, she fell down in other results categories at her level, including

- *Driving sales growth without regard for the capability of the other functions, particularly Operations, to respond. She didn't seek her peers' view of how much sales growth the business could handle. She never bothered to learn what the other functions could do, what their plans were, and what challenges they faced. Her marketing strategy didn't really help the overall business.*

- *Focusing her team's coaching and development on technical skills, to the exclusion of helping them develop leadership skills. As a result, her people weren't promotable, and she didn't have a successor. She was working at the level of a Manager of Others (first-line manager) and not at Function Manager level.*

- *Making assumptions about how the Finance function worked based on her experience in other companies. BRC's Finance function had much more rigorous risk-management procedures and took the time to do more credit checks, to set up automated processing, and to adjust forecasts based on changes in ordering patterns. They were more sophisticated and needed better communication from Chris. The Finance Officer scheduled meetings with her, but she cancelled most of them in favor of last-minute customer calls.*

- *Filling her calendar with customer visits and cold calls. There wasn't much time left over for relationship-building internally, for researching the state of the art, or for helping her boss and business succeed.*

After getting some guidance on how to improve this situation, Chris met with her peers one-on-one and asked them what they needed from her that they weren't getting. She did the same with her direct reports. With her peers she asked for substantial details about their organization and how it worked. Armed with an eye-opening list of needs, she reviewed another company's performance standards (sanitized to avoid disclosing the company's name) for a Function Manager. These standards served as a catalyst for rethinking her entire job and provided guidance for how to express the contributions she needed to make. Specific contributions in leadership, management, and relationships were spelled out and reviewed by peers and subordinates and her boss. A fundamental redesign of her calendar was required and with it some important delegation.

This example was included to illustrate how even "excellent performers" are limited by what they don't know. When properly guided and informed, they react constructively.

Critical Results That Underpin Strategy

While some Function Managers recognize the need to deliver a competitive advantage for the business, many fall short because they haven't produced the underlying results. Some of the most important underlying results are competitive analysis, knowledge of the state of the art, a high-performing organization, a work environment that supports innovation, and a multifunctional thought process. Let's examine each of these results categories and the factors that can help Function Managers deliver these results effectively.

Competitive Analysis

Function Managers generally do a good job when it comes to some of this category's requirements—competitive research for both marketing and sales and customer research involving pricing, product offerings, and advertising are usually handled well. Function Managers also make sure they learn about manufacturing methods, use of technology, and development processes, even though these efforts require a bit more work. Function Managers don't always deliver results, though, when it comes to the human side of the business (except for comparisons of salaries and wages through surveys). They often are in the dark on what competitors are doing in recruiting, training, succession planning, development, and coaching. Finance Function Managers, too, are often unaware of other companies' innovations in the financial arena, and given how important that knowledge is for competitive advantage, this is a significant performance failure. Collecting all these forms of information and producing a competitive analysis is the starting point for developing a functional strategy.

Knowledge of the State of the Art

Working at the state of the art may not be possible because of cost, talent, or other factors, but opting out of state-of-the-art work should be a conscious choice rather than the result of ignorance. Attendance at industry conferences, employment interviews, trade periodicals, and technical discussion forums all provide a glimpse of the leading edge. Experts can be a terrific source for cutting-edge trends and developments but aren't enough by themselves. Since functions comprise many elements, each may have its own leading edge, so the state of the art isn't likely to be one thing. A mistake

Function Managers make is to concentrate their attention on the one thing "making a lot of noise" in the industry. Competitive research and state-of-the-art awareness should work together to shape a Function Manager's thinking. Competitive advantage comes from being better than your current and likely future competitors, but that may yet be a good distance away from the state of the art. Function Managers that deliver in this area display good judgment, choosing the right positioning based on their depth and breadth of knowledge.

High-Performing Organization

Building a high-performing organization is the toughest aspect of a Function Manager's job. The popular misconception is that superior technical or professional capability will deliver the competitive advantage. Technical talent won't shine, however, unless Function Managers give people the opportunity and incentive to use this talent. Because many leaders at lower levels do technical work themselves rather than lead, setting the performance standards bar at world-class level or at least "competitive advantage" level is crucial for reinforcing management and leadership. Function Managers must define, communicate, and enforce these standards. This is what great function leaders do—they teach, give feedback, and coach with these standards in mind. They also prepare at least one of their people to move up to Function Manager, given the importance of succession planning for high-performing organizations.

Work Climate That Supports Innovation

Within the functions is where most innovation occurs, often at the lowest levels. Function Managers must communicate that innovation is expected throughout the function and not just at the lower or upper levels. The performance standards and the management capability must enable them in this regard. Managers have to give their people room to try new things even if the new things aren't successful. Tolerance for mistakes (but not for failure) is required for innovation to have a chance. If mistakes are punished, no one will try anything new. Function Managers, through their actions, create the work climate that supports innovation. These actions can include a generous budget for trying new things, a tolerance for some mistakes, and personal support of their people's efforts. Setting the parameters for innovation through the functional strategy is also a key requirement. Perhaps the most powerful ingredient is requiring all staff to improve what they do, not just repeat what they did yesterday.

Multifunctional Thought Process

Function Managers are members of a multifunctional team; their peers run different functions. To be an effective team, multifunctional thinking is essential. The vast majority of Function Managers have worked only in their current function. While they aren't completely ignorant of the work done in the other functions, they aren't knowledgeable enough in most instances to be true partners. Knowledge of the results, plans, and methods of the other functions, though, makes it possible to develop a multifunctional thought process. Function Managers who make the best decisions and achieve the most ambitious goals are those who take their impact on the other functions into account. Consultation with peers before decisions are made helps. Success of the business, not just the function, is the goal. A multifunctional thought process enables the high level of integration required for business success. For most Function Managers, this is a new and difficult requirement, which didn't exist in their previous jobs.

Functional Strategy Pulls It All Together

Functional strategy is the vehicle for pulling together a broad range of elements that are new when working at this layer. Function

Managers support the business by defining how Business Results will actually be delivered, and how competitive advantage will be achieved. The supporting platform for achieving business strategy, in concert with the others functions, is built on positioning relative to the state of the art, competitive analysis, innovation, and organization effectiveness. While defining the function's future direction—and the plans to achieve it—will benefit everyone in a function, the real beneficiaries are the definers themselves, the Function Managers. At the same time, leaders at lower layers need the functional strategy for setting priorities, giving work direction, and enabling alignment. And leaders in other functions benefit as well from the knowledge.

What the Function Manager must deliver

- Competitive analysis—products and key processes

- Knowledge of the state of the art—multidimensional information

- A functional strategy—leading to competitive advantage

- A climate for innovation—continuous improvement

- High-performing organization—both technical and leadership

- Multifunctional thought process—effective business team membership

What the Function Manager enables

- Clear picture of where the business is going— connecting the function to the business

- Clear understanding of the function's direction—everyone knows where the work is headed

- An environment that supports innovation—including resources and support

- Effective management and leadership—clear priorities and regular feedback

- Resources for obtaining and developing technical and professional talent—time and money

- A model of multifunctional thinking—as many multifunctional thinkers as needed

How Function Managers Hurt the Business

Function Managers actually deliver the Business Results. Responsibility for products, customers, people, and money rests with them. When Function Managers pursue any other agenda, the business suffers, and it often suffers badly. Here are the red flags for Function Managers:

Technical results only. Function Managers shortchange the business when they spend an inordinate amount of time and energy on technical results by solving all the tough technical problems. They got promoted because of their technical prowess and don't want to let go of it. It is their security blanket. While this expertise is useful, it can cause them to become buried in the here and now. Time and attention required for working on the future are diverted to solving today's problems. Meanwhile, the layers below don't learn to solve these problems on their own and remain dependent on the Function Manager's technical expertise. Solving the occasional problem with an emphasis on teaching is useful, but solving most of the problems without teaching is not.

Functional membership. "Functional membership"—roughly translated as being one of the guys or gals—leads to bad decisions.

People are proud of their functional expertise and years of service in the function, so it's natural to want to be in the club. Function Managers, however, need true objectivity when assessing the function's strengths and weaknesses, when deciding what stays and what goes, and in selecting talent. Certainly frequent engagement is necessary for staying abreast of progress or failures, for coaching and for communicating. While it's useful to spend time with people in the function, Function Managers must be ahead of them rather than among them. They must be engaged with people above them and externally. If there is a default position, it should be "out in front," working on the future and understanding competition and the state of the art, not within the function, solving technical problems. Functional membership is the condition I see most frequently. It is a sign that the Function Manager has not transitioned properly to the layer.

Isolation. Function Managers can become isolated from the Business Manager and from peers who run the other functions. The reasons for this isolating tendency vary by function—the Marketing Manager is always with customers; the Engineering Manager is in the lab working on new technology; the Finance Manager works long and late doing analysis; and so on. Certainly there are times when some of this is justifiable, but connecting with the boss and with peers (other than just at staff meetings) helps Function Managers keep a business focus for themselves and their organizations. Functional work for its own sake isn't as useful as functional work that connects well with other functions to deliver the business strategy. In fact, functional work that doesn't support the business strategy leads to failure for Function Managers. It is discouraging to see how much functional isolation exists despite all the literature and accumulated knowledge on the value of collaboration and teamwork. Balanced engagement by the Business Manager is needed; all Function Managers should get time and attention.

Concrete layer. Of all the red flags, a "concrete layer" may be the most alarming. By concrete layer, I mean barriers in an organization that impede both the downward and upward flow of information, ideas, plans, issues, problems, and the like. Frequently those most responsible are in the layer just below Function Manager—the Manager of Managers group. Progress on and commitment to new ideas or changes of any kind is much slower than it should be. True problems don't surface in a timely way. Function Managers must build teams that are committed to the bigger picture—Business Results—not just their own selfish functional interests. Function Managers must confront those who block progress. Concrete layers exist only if leaders allow them to exist. The worst-case scenario is when Function Managers become part of the concrete layer. Their isolation and disagreement with the direction of the business are two common causes of this scenario. Feeling underappreciated or mistreated by the Business Manager or peers also leads to this condition. Function Managers need to be particularly sensitive to the possibility that a concrete layer exists or is being created, their responsibility for contributing to it, and how to remove it.

Putting Results into Practice

Now I'd like to demonstrate how awareness of these critical results—both delivered and enabled—provides organizations with a leg up on improving performance.

A consumer goods company built its performance pipeline to help drive efficiency by improving teamwork and requiring functional integration. The Marketing and Sales functions had been highly valued and rewarded while support functions were given short shrift. Table 5.1 portrays the company's view of required performance for Function Managers. Because it produced and sold fast-moving consumer goods, it needed an organization with alignment and rhythm. Many of the performance standards it chose

Table 5.1 Fast-Moving Consumer Goods Company, Function Manager (Marketing, Finance, IT, Operations, Legal, and so on)

Performance Dimensions	Required Work Values	Full Performance
Operational Results • Total Functional Results Per Company Plan • Consolidated Functional Budgeted Results • Functional Productivity Gains	• Total Business results. • Total Functional results.	• Meets all functional requirements in ways that enable appropriate business results and meets the needs of other functions. • Optimizes/Improves systems and processes in ways that deliver productivity gains. • Makes decisions which are in best interest of the business before consideration of self, own function or market. Prepared to make appropriate trade-offs in interests of bigger business goals.
Leadership Results • Functional Leadership Pipeline • Organizational Development/Self-Sustaining Organization • Change Management (Culture Supporting Strategy) • Functional Strategy supporting Business Strategy • Line of Sight (Functional Vision Aligned with Business Vision) • People engagement & inspiration	• Functional strategy, tied to business. • Functional leadership pipeline. • Functional excellence.	• Develops functional strategy that fully supports business strategy and needs of other functions. • Develops a stream of functional innovation that drives the business forward. • Produces written development plans for self and direct reports; requires direct reports to do the same. Proactively follows-up the plans. • Leads and builds enthusiasm for change. • Actively coaches at every opportunity. • Shows high self awareness of their leadership role. Lives the Guiding Principles consistently. • Takes into account the competition and external developments in producing and developing both standards and programs. • Values and builds diverse teams. • Builds effective leadership pipeline, and robust succession. • Retains talent in the organization. • Engages his/her team in pursuing agreed strategy & plans.

(Continued)

Table 5.1 (Continued)

Performance Dimensions	Required Work Values	Full Performance
Management Results • Functional Plan—Develop, Monitor, and Report • Functional Performance Standards • Key Project Sponsorship • Function Organization/Staffing • Process Definition/Work Processes	• Delegating management of the function to direct reports. • Functional management, at all layers. • Functional efficiency.	• Produces all functional work on time at desired quality level and cost. • Delegates oversight of functional tasks to direct reports. • Develops appropriate measurements and makes them clear to everyone. • Sets priorities in best interest of the business; resolves any conflict promptly. • Ensures process optimization instead of functional excellence for its own sake. • Enables his/her team by providing development opportunities, & implementing the required support systems (HR/IT/Fin).
Relationship Results • Knowledge Sharing—Peers • Cross-Functional Influence • Internal—Up and Down • Functional Chain of Command Vendors/Suppliers/Contractors/ • Business Partners	• Multi-functional relationships. • Vertical relationships.	• Shares information and ideas with other functions; focuses on total business. • Allocates/gives up functional resources to support company goals. • Creates a climate of teamwork and cross-functional cooperation throughout the function.
Innovation (Internal & External) Results • New Ways and Smarter Ways of Doing Old and New Work • External Functional Network	• Functional state of the art—in pursuit of business results.	• Seeks and utilizes customer input in design of services/programs/products. • Exceeds norms in product and service quality. Continuous improvement is the norm. • Proactively listens and engages with internal and external functional network, across markets.

were focused on Function Managers supporting other functions, integrating their work, or enabling other functions to succeed. The very first standard, "Meets all functional requirements in ways that enable appropriate Business Results and meets the needs of other functions," set the tone. This company wanted Business Results delivered through functions that collaborate (rather than compete with or ignore each other) while focusing on business outcomes.

This fast-moving consumer goods company understands that Function Managers need to do the basics of good leadership and manage within the context of business success, not just functional success. Engaging the workforce, innovating, developing people, setting priorities, sharing information, measuring themselves on business success, and building cross-functional teamwork are all part of success. By using the standards properly, the company has made it clear that Function Managers should not be engaged in activities or pursuing results that hurt or inhibit the success of the business or of other functions. In order to get the efficiency and effectiveness required to supply fast-moving goods at the right time and place, they need a common focus (Business Results), teamwork (caring about the success of other functions), and getting everyone in the function on the same page (delegation, communication).

Pay special attention to the "Required Work Values" column in Table 5.1, since these values are especially important for Function Managers here. Valuing the work to be done at this layer more than other work from previous layers is a key for strong results. This company felt that being explicit about work values required for specific results would have a major impact on its Function Managers. Not every company, when creating a performance pipeline, is this specific in the work values area. Here, though, this consumer goods company wanted to get its Function Managers' attention, and this emphasis on values did the trick.

6

Managers of Managers
Productivity

Of all the layers, this one generates the most confusion and requests for clarification. One problem is that people treat the Manager of Managers (MOM) layer as if it were the layer below—Manager of Others. MOMs in every company are responsible for 90–95 percent of the workforce; the layers above them are sparsely populated, relatively speaking. Despite this great responsibility, Managers of Managers are often thought of as "junior" or "unimportant," and that is a second problem.

In fact, Managers of Managers are the key to a productive organization. In difficult business climates where cutbacks and staff reductions are common, they provide the day-to-day thinking, planning, and leading that keep the business on track. Their ability to schedule and organize the work, their skill at breaking through silo walls so that work can flow easily and quickly, their dedication to training and developing the Managers of Others—all these tasks determine how well the business will execute. More specifically, MOMs must achieve and enable critical results and avoid focusing on inappropriate ones. We'll discuss all these results, but first let's profile the Manager of Managers level.

Who Is a Manager of Managers?

Typically, Managers of Managers report to Function Managers and have Managers of Others reporting to them. Many variations of this reporting structure, which is a third problem, cause a good deal of the confusion about MOMs, which I alluded to earlier. Starting from the bottom up, there may be a combination of Managers of Others and Self-Managers (individual contributors) that reports to a MOM. In that case, MOMS should devote most of their time and effort toward dealing with Managers of Others. If guiding the Self-Managers takes most of the time and effort, then such MOMs really should be treated as operating at the Manager of Others level.

In very large organizations, two or more layers of Managers of Managers may be found; for example, large data-processing organizations frequently have two layers of MOMs. Be aware that the critical results are similar for both MOM groups with one proviso: the upper level of MOMs leads the lower layer of MOMs but typically doesn't directly manage the Managers of Others, especially when this dual grouping exists in large organizations.

In small enterprises, some smaller businesses, and in functions like Human Resources and Marketing, MOMs may be absent. In these situations, the Function Manager produces the results normally assigned to MOMs. It is equally likely that in small businesses where the founder is CEO and Business Manager, those reporting to the founder are doing MOM work, not Function Manager work. The founder/CEO in a small company often makes all the product and customer decisions, signs every check as a CFO would do, and complains about being overworked. In those cases the direct reports need to step up to Function Manager work.

Other Sources of Confusion About MOMs

Additional points of confusion about this role come from a few important but somewhat subtle differences from the Manager of Others position:

- Managers of Managers should delegate authority for day-to-day priority setting and other decision making to their direct reports, the Managers of Others. MOMs learned how to delegate tasks, not authority when they were Managers of Others. Often they continue delegating tasks, so that the Managers of Others have no authority—and their people know it. Self-Managers start going directly to the Manager of Managers for needed permission or variances to get their work done.

- Managers of Managers should ask management questions but have only learned to ask task questions. "When will the sale be closed?" is a task question. "What has to be done to make sure your organization can close sales promptly?" is a management question. When Managers of Others are asked task questions, it tends to push them into the tasks.

- Managers of Managers are supposed to work with their peers to produce a lateral flow of work, information, ideas, and so on, but they don't know their peers or don't respect their peers. So they take problems to their boss, not to their peers. That pulls the Function Manager down to a lower layer of work and pushes the MOM down as well.

- Managers of Managers are trained with generic management training, not MOM-specific training. Differences from the previous layer aren't made apparent in the training, so they do now what they did previously.

- Managers of Managers got the job on the basis of the results produced as a Manager of Others, not on their management skills. Results may have been produced because they personally produced them.

Critical Results Needed from MOMs

One reason productivity is so elusive in many companies is that MOMs aren't asked to do enough about it. Function Managers are asked to drive productivity, but they are too far removed from the day-to-day tasks to have a major impact. MOMs, on the other hand, are closer to the work yet not personally responsible for it; this provides them with the proximity and the objectivity necessary to make astute decisions about productivity issues.

Unfortunately, higher-level managers often treat MOMs as if they were Managers of Others, preventing them from participating sufficiently in running the function on a day-to-day basis. It is quite common for MOMs to be excluded from both strategic and operational planning for the function. When they are excluded in this way, they spend a great deal of their time tending to daily tasks and substituting for Managers of Others. They also miss out on learning from the discussion. In these instances, MOMs don't grow their skills sufficiently beyond those of a Manager of Others. I have seen this problem in old-line electric utilities and new software producers.

MOMs should develop two-year operating plans to increase productivity. By creating a climate of acceptance for management work, MOMs help new managers understand their role and speed up the response to management directives. Trained Managers of Others are needed for building that climate and executing that two-year plan. MOMs also need to achieve operational discipline, that is, make sure the processes that are approved for use are followed by everyone, things are done on time, people show up for meetings, and so on. Managers of Managers have to focus on maintaining a good balance of speed and quality of output, and this can only be done if they are enabled sufficiently with information, ideas, customer concerns, and firsthand knowledge of the function's strategy and why it was chosen. It starts with their own team and expands across all relevant peer organizations. Sound working relationships with peers across all functions and with their direct reports as well as with suppliers and customers enable the desired pace. In fact, establishing and maintaining great working relationships with as many peers as possible should be a high priority for MOMs.

Two-Year Operating Plan

Many MOMs work with one-year planning horizons, and this is a major error when it comes to performance. When they are treated as Managers of Others, they are asked to focus on results within this shorter time frame. If, however, an organization wants its MOMs to orchestrate major productivity improvements, they must formalize a longer time frame, as the following example suggests.

Example—Scheduled Maintenance Shutdown

Sarah was promoted to Power Station Manager at a large electric utility. The power station was remotely located, and so she was somewhat isolated from her boss and other leaders. She was one of the first females to run a power station who didn't have an engineering degree. She had been a business major and saw herself as a leader. Making a strong statement through her performance, using business and leadership skills rather than technical know-how to achieve desired objectives, was a personal goal.

Positions like hers are measured on productivity, that is, kilowatt-hours of electricity produced per day. Thus, a normal but costly requirement, such as shutting down the generators for scheduled maintenance to avoid equipment failure, reduced productivity. Four one-week shutdowns per year was the normal schedule for preventative maintenance. Sarah thought about the impact that had on productivity from a Manager-of-Managers perspective. Rather than focus on a shorter time frame as a Manager of Others would, Sarah used her business background and extended the planning horizon to two years. Her calculations suggested that moving the scheduled shutdown weeks for maintenance further apart by paying more attention to the condition of the equipment, she could reduce the number of shutdown weeks from four to three in the first year (though keeping them at four for the second year). This model was soon copied at other power stations. After more experimentation with the interval between shutdowns and the quality of inspections, three shutdowns per year with closer inspection became the standard everywhere.

Sarah was thinking about issues from the right performance leadership level. At this level, many operating problems don't lend themselves to solutions based on annual plans or annual thinking. Process changes, supply chain redefinition, and information technology are examples. In fact, a two-year planning horizon may not be enough for addressing them. MOMs need to be capable of looking at the problems and opportunities they face from at least a two-year perspective, despite all the short-term pressures they face.

Climate of Acceptance for Management Work

This is a result that often slips through the cracks, in large part because it's an intangible, making quantifying tasks and achievements challenging. Yet at the MOM level it is a crucial performance requirement, given the age in which we live. In movies, TV shows, and comic strips, management and managers are portrayed as jokes. The media, too, has written a sufficient number of negative articles about CEOs and other leaders to bolster the perception that managers aren't to be trusted—a perception that exists internally as well as externally. Profound cynicism about the capability of management is readily apparent in many companies. Managers of Managers, however, can moderate or even dissipate much of this cynicism by the leadership tone they set. By demanding full management performance and enabling Managers of Others to perform, they embed a positive attitude. By insisting that the Managers of Others give their people clear work direction, timely and constructive feedback, training and support, reasons behind decisions, and timely problem solving make clear the value of good management. People get conditioned to expect management actions to be beneficial.

Managers of Managers start setting the tone by selecting the right people for management positions. Promoting people who want to lead to the Manager of Others positions and teaching them how to lead is what's needed. Promoting the best technicians, then allowing those persons to do primarily technical and professional work, however, does *not* set the right tone. Instead, it creates a situation where there is one highly productive technical/ professional person (the Manager of Others) and half a dozen unsupervised Self-Managers. Productivity truly suffers. So does the concept of management. "Manager" becomes a status definition (I am higher up than you), not a set of results appropriate to this leadership level.

Building a climate of acceptance for management work helps new managers appreciate and accept their role requirements. Establishing the Manager of Others as a capable leader and the true source of direction, information, advice, and coaching makes a climate of acceptance possible. Steady business rhythm should start right here!

Operational Discipline

Keeping the organization connected so that product changes, new initiatives, special requests, and the like don't fall through the cracks is an important Manager of Managers' responsibility. Getting the right things done in the right way at the right time could be the motto for all MOMs. More than one Manager of Managers has adopted the attitude that "the meeting can't start without me." This entitled mind-set is antithetical to generating necessary results at this level. Showing up on time for meetings properly prepared might seem like a small thing, but it has a big impact on values adopted by managers one level down, not to mention the time wasted when a MOM is routinely late by fifteen minutes or more. Because Managers of Others can be somewhat reticent about imposing operational discipline on their teams, MOMs must make this expectation clear.

At a time when many businesses want to innovate and managers want to break the rules in order to experiment, operational discipline is crucial. As commendable as risk-taking is, managers need to grasp the established policies and processes before they attempt to change them or abandon them. Without this knowledge, these managers become haphazard risk-takers rather than thoughtful innovators. Disconnection is a real danger when every manager does his own thing. MOMs are in charge of making sure work proceeds in a logical, connected fashion, and imposing operational discipline helps in this regard. Balancing the desire to innovate with the need to deliver requires clear thinking and good judgment by Managers of Managers.

Free Flow of Work, Information, Ideas

Silo-busting is done best at this level. Political problems that impede progress at higher levels are usually subordinated to practical considerations here. MOMs, therefore, are in pivotal positions when it comes to work and information flow. They need to understand where their work comes from and where it goes so they can create connections and give or receive feedback. Mistakes can be reduced and repetition of mistakes eliminated if the proper dialogue takes place at MOM layers across the business or enterprise. The most productive MOMs reach out regularly to learn what's coming and when, and to learn what recipients think of the MOMs' work product.

Great Relationships in All Directions

MOMs should be engaged with people much more than with technology or tasks. I cannot overemphasize the importance of establishing strong people connections at this level. It starts with the Function Manager (what is the function strategy? what are the priorities?), extends to his team (here is what we have to deliver and when), reaches laterally to peers (what's coming? how are we doing?), and includes suppliers and customers (here's what we need; what do you expect?). While it is time consuming, building great relationships make productivity possible. ("I know Charlie in Accounting, quite well. He'll put a rush on the analysis we need.") MOMs who are pulled down one layer to backfill for weak Managers of Others, or pushed down one layer by Function Managers who won't work at the right level, don't have time to build the right relationships, or plan, or bust silos. When these MOMs are working at the wrong level, productivity always suffers.

Getting the Best Leadership ROI

Successful MOMs create leverage. By developing better and better plans and growing effective Managers of Others, they can drive more and more production or output with the same or fewer resources (input). This leverage is an important source of productivity improvement. Good Managers of Others enable the Self-Managers to produce effectively. In difficult times, if there is only one dollar to spend on developing leaders, spend it on Managers of Managers. They produce the best short-term return. If you invest that dollar higher up, you get a future return, which could arrive too late to save your business.

What the Manager of Managers must deliver

- Two-year operating plan

- Climate of acceptance for management work

- Trained Managers of Others

- Flow of work and information

- Relationships up, down, and across

- Leverage

- Discipline

What the Manager of Managers enables

- Clear direction

- Priorities

- Right person in right job

- Speed of decision making

- Critical connections

- Feedback from those who receive the work

- High-performance work environment

Example—Helping MOMs Understand Their Roles

A leading biotechnology company, let's call it Biotech 123, was experiencing rapid sales growth driven by some breakthrough products. To support this growth, Biotech 123 hired a great deal of new technical talent, and many Managers of Others and MOM-level leaders. New technical people brought their own ideas of what should be done and how to do it. Since the new leaders came from many different places, they all had different ways of leading and managing. As you might expect, many of the new MOMs were struggling because they were working at the wrong level. It was hard for them to get role clarity in the midst of this rapid growth. Senior management decided to construct a performance pipeline to establish role clarity, especially at the MOM level.

One of Biotech 123's first steps involved work interviews to find out exactly what was being done and what wasn't being done at the lower layers. They discovered that 75 percent of Managers of Managers' work actually involved Manager of Others' tasks. They were directly supervising Self-Managers in their organization, giving feedback to Self-Managers, producing weekly work plans, and analyzing field-test data for accuracy.

As Biotech 123 created their pipeline, they spelled out expected results at different managerial levels, full performance standards, required competencies, and indication of wrong performance (Table 6.1). Making clear what was to be worked on and the standards for full performance were essential to role clarity. The competencies were included to help MOMs plan development for themselves as well as guide the Function Manager on what development might be needed. In the table, you'll notice the column titled, "Indicators of Need to Develop." This variation in the usual Pipeline model was included because Biotech 123 wanted a method for conveying unacceptable activity. They wanted to communicate what managers should stop doing clearly enough to enable self-correction.

Biotech 123 found a significant gap between the results their managers were delivering and those that they should have been delivering. For this reason, they used their pipeline as a training framework for all MOMs. This training turned out to be highly effective, in large part because these newly hired Managers of Managers wanted to do the right thing; they just didn't know what it was at Biotech 123. The biggest training challenge was teaching them how to choose and develop Managers of Others. MOMs had a strong technical orientation and tended to select for technical skills and coach for technical results. Given Biotech 123's strong scientific focus, this technical emphasis was understandable and

Table 6.1 Biotechnology Company, Manager of Managers

Required Work Values
- Getting results through managers
- Developing leaders
- Integrating with other units
- Productivity
- Trade-off decisions

Result Area	Full Performance	Required Behaviors and Competencies	Indicators of Need to Develop
Technical/Professional/ Operational Deliver Program/Project Right Science Dose Optimization Molecule Committee membership Protocol for Trials Financial Management (budget) Vendor Management Branding Communication Outsourcing Final Study Reports Program feasibility	• Met both individual and aggregate goals and makes appropriate adjustments • Trade-off decisions improved over all 1 results for current year and next • Provided science coaching to assure achievement of goals and results • Research information delivered to strategy makers • Contributed to relevant strategy and drove its execution	• Sets own and team' goals with relevant metrics that are challenging but achievable • Maintains persistence in the face of highly complex and/or adverse circumstances • Contributes to the business planning process • Identifies and uses key financial indicators necessary to measure business performance • Aligns relevant plans for own area with company-wide strategy, adapting these as needed	• Doesn't have time for thinking and reflecting, as still involved in reviewing daily activities or performing an individual contributor role • May be reluctant to communicate bad news

Leadership

- Communicate Vision and Purpose
- Model behavior
- Succession Planning
- Inform upward and across
- Coaching/Develop/Bring out the Best
- Right leader in the right job
- Make people successful
- Strategic input (to programming)

- All department members understand and support the vision and the strategy
- Lead by example; lives the values
- Future leaders and future managers of managers identified and developed
- Models and builds enthusiasm for change

- Builds capacity for replicable execution in business performance, not just isolated victories
- Fosters change and creativity by championing new and better ways to do things and making it safe for others to do so
- Clarifies peoples' roles in change efforts and sets clear targets that focus and align people effectively
- Aligns short-term development goals with peoples' longer-term aspirations and company's business needs
- Articulates what specifically is required for people to advance to the next level
- Adapts coaching style to meet the unique needs of the individual or situation
- Hires/selects the best people for both current and potential roles

- Not devoting enough time to coaching of managers and role modeling feedback and accountability
- May prioritize time with peer managers at the expense of coaching time with managers in development
- Hoards talent
- May select managers based on technical/functional expertise

Management

- Make decisions
- Delegate
- Quality guidance
- Planning, priorities and trade-offs
- React to problems
- Performance measurement and rewards
- Productivity
- Information Flow
- Growth and scalability
- Integration with own and other groups

- Improved processes increased productivity
- First-line managers held accountable for management work; coached and developed
- Team focused on key priorities/projects; measures and milestones ensure things happen as planned
- Hard decisions made promptly, even when they may be unpopular
- Cross-functional team-work drives business integration and performance delivery
- Delegation and prioritization creates time for thinking and longer term planning

- Maintains a positive culture of accountability in work areas, such as by clarifying accountabilities and following up regularly and constructively
- Adapts operational processes for greater alignment with other processes
- Determines roles and responsibilities for individuals and teams
- Determines systems, standards, and assumptions that apply to an individual, team of group
- Capitalizes on every opportunity to recognize or coach each individual to higher performance
- Conveys unconventional or unpopular points of view constructively
- Modifies team roles and responsibilities to enhance team performance

- Steps in to directly manage when first-line managers get behind schedule
- Doesn't work hard enough at lateral integration
- May rush to blame; may not solve process issues, but resolve incidents only
- May still rescue managers in performance management or missed deliverables

(Continued)

Table 6.1 *(Continued)*

Result Area	Full Performance	Required Behaviors and Competencies	Indicators of Need to Develop
Relationships • Customer • Regulatory • Peers/Other Orgs • Department Collaboration • Awareness of other functions	• Information readily shared with peers, and throughout the function • Managed without boundaries laterally • Multi-functional and/or global thinking evident in plans, programs, procedures • External network produces meaningful benefit of the company	• Develops details understanding of customers' needs, issues, and priorities—consistently searching for ways to improve services to them • Is able to suspend biases and other strongly held beliefs in order to actively listen to others' views • Considers the needs and interests of others and incorporates information relevant to them in communications • Shares expertise with other departments when asked	• Not prioritizing customer or partner interaction; may delegate to others or ignore • May have "telling style" with customer or partners vs. learning or listening • May be impatient with peer meetings and differing needs/ perspectives • No external network
Horizon 20.10.1 • Management and leadership innovation	• New ways to do management work discovered and applied • Takes calculated risks and learns from mistakes to improve results	• Introduces improvements to processes, operations, or practices in own or other areas that yield high value and sustainable business performance • Shows creativity and foresight in applying cross-functional knowledge to arrive at innovative solutions • Takes action—and empowers others as well—to make process improvements that add value through greater reliability or efficiency	• Risk averse, takes no risks • No interest in learning management and leadership skills and practices

necessary, but it was impeding the company's ability to execute its growth strategy.

With the Performance Pipeline standards in hand and training classes completed, several of the MOMs began to spend their time quite differently. Several Managers of Others were moved to Self-Manager positions. Some of the better Managers of Others had their number of direct reports increased. Many requisitions for additional people were rescinded. Function Managers reported receiving more requests for clarification of direction and priorities. While not yet complete, the change was readily apparent.

Results We Don't Want

You would think that Managers of Managers have plenty to do at their own level and that they wouldn't need to look elsewhere for work. When the MOM does the work of a Manager of Others, the Function Manager gets pulled down to the MOM level. This accounts for why many Function Managers hurt their business. MOMs have to help Function Managers by collectively making the function productive in the short term and up to two years out. So the first result that we truly don't want is *causing the Function Manager to do unaddressed MOM work.*

A second unwanted result related to the previous one is the *management of the day-to-day work of technician/professionals.* That's the work of the Manager of Others. Managers of Others don't learn to manage and lead if they aren't required to and have someone else already doing the work. They will revert to the technician/ professional role they held in their previous job. The Self-Manager team figures out quickly who is "in charge" and goes to the person with the answer or the power to get the answer.

A third result we don't want is *short-term planning only.* As I emphasized earlier, a one-year or shorter time frame is unacceptable at this level—a level where many critical improvements or problems demand a longer-term perspective. Also, when MOMs are short-term oriented, they usually aren't prepared to step up to the function layer. They don't develop necessary skills or the right way of looking at the business. Many companies I have worked with lament their lack of bench strength, but what they don't always realize is that allowing MOMs to work and think like Managers of Others diminishes bench strength. The huge skills and work values gaps between MOMs and Function Managers make it difficult to promote MOMs. More MOMs would be promotable if they were required to do the right work, especially long-term work.

Finally, the fourth undesired result is for MOMs to *ask the wrong question*. Asking Managers of Others what they are going to do to speed up production or be sure to meet due dates pushes them to get personally involved in the work. The proper question is about what they will do to make their organization faster, more productive, or more effective. The right questions are whether they need better people, more complete processes, higher standards, a different situation, and so on. Asking the right questions seems to be one of the hardest things for MOMs to learn.

It is fair to say, particularly in uncertain times, that every business and every enterprise would like to be more productive. Effective Managers of Managers are the key, but the job is hard to learn. Some prominent reasons are

- The Function Manager is doing the MOM's work

- MOMs are trained exactly the same as Managers of Others or attend Function Manager courses

- They get promoted for the wrong reason and didn't really learn how to manage other people in their previous position

- They get asked the wrong questions, just as the Managers of Others are frequently asked the wrong questions

- The organization views this job as about the same as a Manager of Others

- Half the direct reports are individual contributors

I have not worked with any company that really has this layer right. You would be safe in assuming things could be done much better in your company. So, invest the time and energy required to understand this layer; select good managers for the positions; teach the differences and, in particular, the subtleties; and be sure your Function Managers are working at the right level.

7

Managers of Others
The Enablers

A bsolutely nothing is more valuable to a Self-Manager (an individual contributor) at work than a good boss. Good bosses make the work experience more pleasant, facilitate completion of tough tasks without undue stress, and answer questions. Ineffective bosses, on the other hand, make the work experience unpleasant, increase stress, and leave people scratching their heads.

From an enterprise perspective, 80 to 90 percent of all employees work for a Manager of Others. So Managers of Others have the most direct impact of all managers on things like morale, motivation, attitude, job satisfaction, quality, and employee retention. An ineffective Manager of Others makes the people under them unhappy, unproductive, and often times resentful. Quality suffers and customers feel the impact.

Managers of Others (MOOs) make the product or service happen. They oversee the actual work at every stage of the process and are responsible for the workforce that actually touches the product or delivers the service. They are accountable for getting the right workers to do the right work in the right way at the right time for the right cost with the right quality. It is not an easy job because they do their work without much say concerning what resources will be available, how much time will be allotted, or what standard should be met. They are the "make it happen" link in the chain but are often required to produce with less support than needed.

All the strengths and weaknesses of the enterprise show up on the MOO's desk. If planning is done well in the enterprise, for example, the resources MOOs need will be there. If recruiting is well done and the enterprise is a good place to work, they will have the people they need. Poor operational planning, ineffective recruiting, and insufficient communication are more common and directly impact the MOOs' ability to deliver. Even the best-run enterprises and businesses have some problems, so the MOOs must be resourceful enough to overcome the problems and deliver the product or service. Getting a good result for customers often comes down to the ingenuity of the MOOs and their teams. I'll follow the same format as the previous chapters, focusing on the critical underlying results, the full job, and results MOOs should not deliver. The composition of the team to be managed varies greatly at the Manager of Others level; I'll emphasize this point later in the chapter and examine the implications.

Critical Underlying Results

When you think about Managers of Others, you probably think of supervising, coaching, giving feedback, and the like. Those are the inputs they make. In this chapter, I focus on the output, the results they need to deliver.

Delivering the right product or service to the customer at the right cost and quality is an outcome built on several critical underlying results. These underlying results collectively provide the framework for high performance by the individual contributors. While there are many results to be delivered by this layer, the following seem to make the most difference and should have highest priority:

- Context

- Connection

- Team capability

- Completion

- Balanced caring

- Management skills

Example

Rita was a Business Development Specialist in a small insurance company; this was her first job after graduating as a marketing major. She had been employed there for a few months and was growing increasingly frustrated.

Her boss, Joe, spent most of his time either calling on customers or analyzing sales and market data. Other Business Development Specialists, her peer group, were also frequently out of the office calling on customers. As a result, Rita couldn't get anyone on the team or her boss to help her learn the ropes. She spent her time studying the market, learning about the competition, and educating herself about the company's products and their sales process. Waiting for Joe to help her develop the necessary knowledge and skills seemed like a path of failure, so Rita taught herself the basics of the job.

After six months of learning and calling on customers in the market segment assigned to her, Rita came up with a new product idea. She presented it to Joe with great enthusiasm. He said he would take it up to senior management. She asked if she could present it to them but was told that they didn't know her; Joe said he would present it.

After waiting for three weeks, Rita got her answer. Joe said that senior management felt that the product didn't fit the strategy. Rita asked him what the strategy was. Joe said the strategy was to accelerate growth by introducing new products and entering new markets. She asked him what the parameters were and was told that a new product had to be "liked" by the CEO.

After hearing that response, Rita started looking for a new job. She resigned the next week.

That was the right thing for Rita to do. Joe failed to provide Rita with the first of our MOO results requirements: context. No one helped her to hit the ground running. No one gave her the lay of the land, explaining "how we get things done around here." No one provided her with insight about how to move new product ideas through the system. So instead of maximizing the value of a new employee with high potential, Joe—specifically his failure to deliver this result at his managerial level—drove Rita out of the company.

Context

When individual contributors show up for work on day one, they need everything required to get their job done. They must have a job definition, tools for doing the work, information about what to do, a sense of the boundaries (such as rules and standards), work priorities, and many other things. Effective Managers of Others provide all this so that it makes sense to the new person. They don't simply dump everything on new hires and overwhelm them but cluster and sequence information so that it can be absorbed easily.

Realistically, though, MOOs have to recognize that whatever they tell their new people will be filtered through what coworkers tell them. Coworkers will add their spin to the information, which may be quite different from what the bosses say. For instance, "Don't work too hard; it's not worth it," or "This is a bad boss; don't do as she says." In order to help new hires make sense of it all, the boss provides context. Context gives these starting employees a framework to help them think and act in the appropriate way. Context includes a combination of the enterprise's purpose, the state-of-the-business and function, and the purpose of the unit. It directs the person's energy and helps overcome the conflicting picture that comes from the new person's peers. It can sound something like, "We have to meet or beat every delivery date because our company wants to maintain its position as the number one service provider, but this business has been missing its delivery dates. We all have to pitch in and try a little harder."

MOOs recognize that what might be obvious to them or their bosses may not be obvious to individual contributors, particularly new ones. MOOs are privy to reports and other information that can help them provide the context that is otherwise invisible to neophytes. This information enables individual contributors to start to self-manage. Having a context makes it possible to build the right judgment and make the right choices so that the right things get done.

Connection

MOOs create several different kinds of connections for their people and for themselves. First, these connections are rooted in a clear sense of the value that the enterprise adds. Managers at every level require a positive view of the company and what it stands for, and a willingness to express that view to the people around them; the ability to act on that view means making sure things work properly. Second, they must connect their team to the company and to each other so that they can work together to deliver the value. This connecting goes beyond teamwork to a commitment to do what's needed to help the enterprise succeed; doing extra for the company's benefit is also part of it—for example, "I know it's quitting time, but I really must finish this report [or this repair or this customer service requirement] because the Business Manager needs it today." When Managers of Others do their jobs effectively, employees gain confidence from feeling connected to the team, the business, and the enterprise. Understanding where they fit and how they fit builds connection.

Team Capability

Managers of Others coach and teach their team, and most individual contributors learn their job from their boss. Yet these and other typical MOO tasks aren't really useful unless the outcome is a capable team. Focusing on the end state—team capability—gives the activities more meaning and helps the Manager of Others decide which activity is needed. For the sake of the team, the manager at some point may need to remove or reassign a given employee rather than teach and coach him. For the enterprise and business to succeed, MOOs must deliver the promised value. If coaching and teaching aren't paying off in value creation, then results-producing managers make other choices. Coaching and teaching are important, but productive Managers of Others must sometimes step out of their comfort zones and focus on other tasks. For this reason, MOOs often find producing capability a highly challenging result. Removing or reassigning people is never easy. Getting constant improvement from everyone is also a tough chore. Perhaps the best test of a Manager of Others is the capability she can build. Context and connections are part of it and do help considerably, but a MOO's efforts should culminate in having a team that can deliver under any set of conditions.

Completion

It's not activity that matters; it's results. In other words, what separates good organizations from bad ones is completion: "We don't stop until the job is done and the customer is served." High-performing Managers of Others don't just preside over beehives of activity; they make sure those hives produce honey.

We have all experienced the difference between activity and completion in restaurants. A waiter asks if you would like something to drink. You tell him water will do. Ten minutes later the water isn't on the table. So you ask another waiter to bring some. Maybe it arrives quickly, and maybe it doesn't. So you wonder what these waiters think their job is: just to ask (with a smile, of course), or to ask and deliver, or to ask and deliver promptly. The answer comes from the standard for completion, set by the business or by the Manager of Others, and the enforcement of that standard. It isn't likely that the restaurant has a standard to ask the customer what he wants and then bring it to him if and when you feel like it.

I use a restaurant example because so much of the completion or lack of completion is visible to us in restaurants. (It is also visible to the restaurant manager!) Office settings have the same need for completion and frequently more serious negative consequences when tasks aren't executed properly. Similarly, most organizations have standards like restaurants, and these standards govern the execution of tasks. Consider such important details as checking the most recent facts to be sure a report is accurate and up to date; getting to root causes rather than responding to superficial symptoms; verifying through additional sources before sending information; considering patients' overall health and removing the sponges before sewing them up. The business and the enterprise experience real problems when tasks aren't completed. Managers of Others are the last line of leadership defense for ensuring that completion is achieved. Completion is a business imperative, not a "nice to have" item.

Balanced Caring

By "balanced" I mean that Managers of Others must find the right mix for how they parcel out their concern for and empathy with others. This can be a challenge on a number of levels. It's sometimes difficult not to play favorites since some managers respond more favorably to certain individuals, not only because of their performance but because of their personalities. MOOs can also find themselves unbalancing the caring equation when they care far more about the organization and too little about their people—or vice versa.

My Mentor, Walt Mahler, thought that managers should develop a "climate of approval." He felt that managers should give their team a sense of confidence by saying, "I approve of you and what you are doing." This is one way to demonstrate balanced caring, and it often results in reciprocal loyalty and caring.

Caring also includes concern for the customer and for the success of the enterprise and the business. Managers of Others are the frontline of support and motivation for employees. In addition, they are the first line of leadership for the success of the enterprise. Balanced caring includes caring about the customer, the people, and the business. All three are better served because of it. When managers lower standards or make excuses for their people, however, their caring has become unbalanced—they are protecting their people at great cost to the business, and customers won't be well served. Certainly not all "caring" managers lower the performance bar, but it happens often enough to be of concern. Favoring one person, too, can harm the functioning of a team, since unfavored members feel they aren't very important; it also makes completion difficult when these "lesser" team members feel the bar should be lowered for them as it has been for the favorite.

Favoring the company over the employee on every occasion is equally bad. Legitimate needs for exceptions exist, and the MOO must exercise judgment. Favoring the customer over the employees and over the business creates unsustainable conditions.

Finally, for an enterprise to be successful, it has to balance the interests of all stakeholders. In particular, the interests of customers, shareholders, employees, and the community have to be addressed. All leaders must learn this balancing act, and it's an easier lesson to learn if they care about all stakeholders and if they inculcate that care at the MOO level.

Management Skills

Managers of Others are the feeder pool for all the other management positions in the business (Corporate Staff can be an exception). Learning the basic skills includes planning, delegating, motivating, coaching, giving feedback, measuring performance, and distributing rewards. Practicing these skills and receiving feedback from the Manager of Managers is the process by which people develop these competences. A quick pass through this layer doesn't make sense, since these skills need to be built in depth and be fully ingrained. Similarly, managers who focus myopically on doing the technical/professional work also miss out on learning a range of managerial skills.

New Managers of Others have a tough transition to make, so they usually don't become effective quickly or without help. Tackling the more subtle but powerful results discussed so far—context, connection, team capability, completion, and balanced caring—requires moving away from a focus on self to focusing on the team, the customers, and the business. Most new managers will remain self-focused until they learn the basics.

It's not just learning this range of managerial skills that takes time but making the "perspective" transition from "one of the gang" to "the boss." Valuing achievement through others rather than just through their own efforts is a major transition, especially for high-achieving individual contributors. Signing up for the status (being the boss) and the work (getting results through others) are critical indicators of success. Learning and embedding managerial skills, therefore, probably won't happen until these two indicators emerge. For this reason, Managers of Managers must monitor their MOOs regularly to understand what progress is being made.

What the Manager of Others must deliver

- Context

- Connection

- Team capability

- Completion

- Balanced caring

- Management skills

What the Manager of Others enables

- Purpose

- Priorities

- Standards

- Judgment

- Development and professional growth

- Rewards and recognition

- Technical/professional results

- Teamwork

- Information at an absorbable rate

A Unique Aspect of the Role

Managers of Others all supervise teams, but the types of teams vary considerably depending on functional responsibility or other factors. Understanding the challenges MOOs face on the basis of these factors provides insight into the specificity of results—the ways different MOOs must tailor their actions and work values to achieve optimum productivity. Let's look at specific MOO subtypes and their teams:

Sales Managers with ten sales professionals often work with a geographically scattered group. Building connection is difficult because the sales team members don't see each other very much. They also are financially motivated to spend as much time as possible on customers and selling rather than on communicating with the boss and colleagues. Because they rely primarily on e-mail and tele-phone to communicate with management and peers, their Sales Managers must build connections for them.

The *Financial Analysis Manager* in a product business who is responsible for three analysts, or a *Corporate Lending Officer* in a banking business who is responsible for a small team, fall into the transactor-manager category. They are doers who provide high-level value. Their teams comprise trained professionals who provide support to their MOO as well as initiate work on their own. Because their people don't expect much traditional managing, they usually find it difficult or unnecessary to focus on the six deliver-ables crucial to results at the MOO level. Special emphasis by their MOM is required to make sure these transactor-managers learn to manage.

Factory Foremen with large numbers of hourly workers don't usually do the work themselves. Their challenge is getting their people to accept the context as defined by the company, not by a third party (such as their union) or by their peers in other parts of the factory. When factory foremen don't become the primary source of communication of the context, low output is the result.

Payroll Managers and *Accounts Payable Managers* have teams composed primarily of clerical workers and a few professionals. The work tends to be routine and repetitive. Completion is often driven by due dates such as payday or bill-paying due dates. Because the work is repetitive and administrative, teams often become bored and stop caring. The challenge for the MOOs is to keep them from getting careless.

An *Engineering Manager* with a team of graduate engineers or a *Research Manager* with a team of scientists has well-educated teams who often don't want much management; many don't need it. Pursuing their profession and applying their training are what drives the individual contributors. Thus, these managers often lack daily opportunities to develop their management skills. The

MOO must make sure timely completion is achieved, not just experimentation.

Sales Call Center Managers or *Customer Service Call Center Managers* may have as many as thirty people on their teams. Typically, these managers rely on phone calls and e-mails to run these teams after their people have been trained. The MOOs may help individual team members with troublesome calls and unusual situations, but they usually struggle to create a sense of connection. Because their people are constantly on the phone and at their work stations, their main connection, literally and figuratively, is with customers. Connection to the enterprise in the face of customer needs and concerns is the MOO's challenge.

Project Managers have a team that changes with every new project. The team works on the project until it is finished, then they move on to another project or back to a functional home base. The Project Manager usually manages the tasks, not the people. Balanced caring is difficult because of the task focus. Learning people development skills is difficult because Project Managers seldom have the time or motivation to develop their temporary team. Project Managers should have more accountability for building capability while the people are assigned to the project rather than simply driving task completion.

Contract workers are becoming a major segment of the workforce. Managing them is different. They may work from home, be employed only for a short time period, and provide specific technical competence not currently found in the company. While they don't receive much attention from management, they need more attention than full-time employees. Context and connection are minimal or missing. Both have to be provided so that the right work gets done in the right way. If there is a chance of longer-term engagement, then building capability is also needed. Using contract workers is likely to remain important; learning to manage them properly so that the right work gets done in the right way will remain important.

Many other situations and challenges exist for Managers of Others besides the eight listed here. For instance, managing a team of railroad train drivers who are constantly in motion, or managing maintenance workers in factories or offices both have connection and capability issues because the team is seldom together and almost never in sight. While team composition should not materially alter the expected results, it will change how those results are achieved and the degree of difficulty of achievement.

The Whole Job

To generate optimum results, Managers of Others must go through a significant shift in work values. In fact, the shift from individual contributor to first-time manager is probably more radical than any other movement from one layer to the next. It is analogous to going from actor to director in movies, or going from player to coach in sports. Both of these analogies help to frame the transition required. The director isn't in the movie but helps the actors deliver great performances. The coach isn't in the game but helps the players become a successful team. In both cases, great individual performances by themselves aren't enough. Audiences must like the movie or it will be a flop; teams must win. Directors and sports coaches have to balance many variables, including who is in the cast or on the team, how well they are learning their roles, how well they are working with the other members of the cast or team, whether they will be ready when they have to be, who needs more of the director's or coach's time, who should be replaced, and so on. First-time managers have never had to deal with these issues before. Even experienced managers struggle with them. Many times, the challenges they pose send neophyte managers back to their individual contributor mind-sets—they long for a time when life was simpler and more fun. In some instances, they revert in practice if not in job responsibility to an individual contributor to fix the problem.

If MOOs are to avoid this possibility, they must understand what performance standards define the "whole job." They need to recognize that there is no going back, either in fact or in attitude; that if they want to be a high-performing Manager of Others, they must grasp, accept, and apply skills appropriate to this level.

To help you understand what the performance standards for doing the whole job are, I've provided three examples.

Table 7.1 is a sample of performance standards that define the "whole job" for the Manager of Others. This particular enterprise comprises many country business units that produce and sell fast-moving consumer goods. Effective execution at a rapid pace is critical to business success, so the Management standards come first. It is also a market-driven business, so there are several references to customers. Since each country has different laws and customs, local compliance is necessary, so a section labeled "CSR" (Country Social Responsibility) is involved.

This company did a particularly good job of defining the required transition in work values. They made it clear that valuing the right work was expected of everyone and was considered to be a critical requirement for sustained success.

Tables 7.2 and 7.3 provide examples of how a resource company differentiated between two different work populations. Table 7.2 has standards for Operational Managers of Others. Their work is almost exclusively on day-to-day production, safety, and teamwork. Table 7.3 has standards for managers of specialists with a team of trained professionals such as engineers or accountants. They focus on the quality of advice or solutions proposed by the team, developing technical skills of their people, and building external relationships important to the profession.

I've included these examples from two different companies to communicate that the performance standards must reflect the nature of the job. At this level, many different populations to manage exist, so different standards are often necessary.

Table 7.1 Manager of Others

Shift in Work Values

- From results through personal effort and cooperation to results through others
- From personal productivity to team productivity and individual productivity
- From working as a member of a team to building an effective and successful team
- From planning own work to planning work for team and performance management
- From valuing professional standards to valuing managerial work
- From developing high-quality individual work and skills to developing managerial skills

Results	Full Performance	Exceptional Performance	Skills, Knowledge, and Experience
Management • Priorities • Work Plans • Execution and process management • Problem solving • Productivity • Compliance (SOX, Audit, local tax and labor legislation, etc) • Project management	• Priorities for self and team established based on department/function objectives • All employees had clear direction, accountability, agreed upon current and measurable objectives • Control system ensured timely results and no surprises • Self & team in full compliance with internal policies, processes, standards and local legislation • Productivity increases each year; Self and team consistently reduced all non-value-adding work and waste	• Management practices copied by peers • Decision making, problem solving and compliance set the standards for peers' teams • Each individual and team in total met all goals	• Sub-function experience & expertise • Organizational and time management skills • Ability to anticipate and avoid problems • Ability to think logically • Ability to make quality decisions • Delegation skills • Full Knowledge of function strategy • Project management skills • Knowledge and interpretation of policies, processes, procedures and systems • Sound judgment *(Continued)*

161

Table 7.1 (Continued)

Results	Full Performance	Exceptional Performance	Skills, Knowledge, and Experience
Professional/Technical/ Operational • KBIs delivery • Sales/volume/cost • Budget and expense management • Customer Satisfaction • Customer/vendor influence and decisions • Information analysis, sharing and reports • Project delivery	• Delivered product, service, advice to specification within budget and on time through team • All mission critical goals/KBIs met • Projects met all targets and helped deliver function strategy* • Customer Satisfaction surveys were analyzed and related action plans were developed • Management of customer (external/internal) engagement process enabled achievement of objectives • Advanced information on professional/ technical/operational opportunities and changes shared appropriately • Right vendor delivered right services at right time for the right price* • Requested reports delivered accurately and on time	• All mission critical goals/KBIs exceeded • New (additional) results achieved within budget • Extra value through customer and vendor partnerships	• General business practices used here • Ability to see the "big picture" • Ability to read and interpret market data and competitive response • Drive for results • Understanding of cost/ revenue impact of decisions

162

People Development
- Team strength
- Team development
- Coaching and feedback
- Successor Development
- Recruiting
- Employee Training

- All team members have and use required technical competence
- Coaching and feedback were part of day-to-day job and there were no surprises in the performance evaluation
- All employees had a current development plan and were actively pursuing it
- Identified successor's development plan was implemented
- Right person in right job to deliver results
- New hires have potential for bigger jobs

- Team members sought by other departments/functions
- Exceptional performers wanted to work on his/her team
- Sought out as coach by other areas

- Identification and selection of talent
- Coaching skills
- Ability to create a learning environment
- Teaching [company] culture requirements
- Feedback skills

Leadership
- Translation of Group/Country/Function strategic guidelines into local/departmental purpose and direction
- Change leadership
- Performance management
- Employee retention
- Motivation/recognition

- Group/Country/Function strategic guidelines were translated into local/departmental goals and direction*
- Need for change was clearly communicated and accepted by the team
- Regular recognition of employees produced increased performance
- Poor performance addressed quickly
- Lives corporate values and Code of Business Conduct

- Considered a role model for leading high-performing and diverse front-line teams
- Team effectiveness was greater than peers'
- Role model for living corporate values and directives at this layer

- Ability to interpret function strategy and culture*
- Ability to implement change*
- Ability to set clear standards for performance
- High integrity
- Ability to adapt leadership style appropriately
- Ability to identify motivators key to individual performance
- Conflict resolution

(Continued)

163

Table 7.1 (*Continued*)

Results	Full Performance	Exceptional Performance	Skills, Knowledge, and Experience
Relationships • Customers/vendors/suppliers • Functional stakeholders (peers, manager, functional community) • Opinion leaders and other important stakeholders • Cross-functional teamwork	• Customers/suppliers/vendors interface included win-win solutions • Open communication with peers and manager(s) assured "no surprises" • Trust and confidence developed with internal stakeholders • Cooperation with other functions ensured improved team's results	• Function relationships enabled country's/BU's/Group's unique needs to be met • Plans and goals reflected multi-unit thinking	• Ability to build relationships that enable results • Ability to communicate effectively • Country/BU business knowledge/awareness • Ability to read the situation and understand priorities • Knowledge of local needs and practices • Teamwork skills and mindset • Ability to develop win/win solutions

Growth and Innovation • New technical/operational/professional initiatives • New ideas • Technical/functional innovation* • Systems, processes and standards improvement	• Track record of improvements driven by curiosity and application of new knowledge and ideas* • Relevant processes/programs continuously improved • Business initiatives were implemented successfully • Team targets were exceeded through finding new ways of using function process/program improvements and new ideas • Continuous improvement was a "way of life" in the team	• Willingness to experiment and try new ideas • Process improvement skills • Product and industry knowledge • Benchmarking of best practices within [enterprise] in own function
CSR • Policy understanding • Health, Safety & Environment • Employer reputation	• CSR strategy and program fully understood and implemented as appropriate by the team • Health, safety & environment management systems and procedures in place and followed • Workplace conditions (physical) supported productivity, health and safety • Ensured that the company's local events enhanced the company's image* • Lives enterprise Citizenship • Opportunities for partnering with the community actively leveraged (e.g. speeches to educational institutions) • CSR programs copied by peers • Role model for enterprise Citizenship in the Country	• Ability to disseminate and enforce health, safety & environment policy • Full knowledge of enterprise policies

*Item is critical to current strategy.

Table 7.2 Manager of Others, Operational

Guiding Principles: (1) Getting results through others. (2) Engaging, training, and serving others. (3) Remove obstacles inhibiting team performance. (4) From teamwork to teambuilding. (5) Taking accountability for success of others. (6) Living and prompting company values. (7) From personal planning to planning for team results. (8) From individual results to providing customer results.

Results	Full Performance	Exceptional Performance
Business, Financial, and Technical Results • Delivery target achievement, e.g., minerals recovered/sorted, tons treated • Cost target achievement • Quality target achievement • Productivity target achievement, e.g., tons per man hour per person, turnaround time	• Targets, due dates and quality standards consistently met by self and team • Produced consistent results by holding employees to agreed-upon targets, methods and measures • Incremental improvement in results achieved through productivity improvement (more with less)	• Targets, due dates and quality standards regularly exceeded • New results in new ways • Set the standard for frontline managers in achieving results • Productivity efficiency and effectiveness increased significantly each year
Leadership & Growth Results • Goal clarity, alignment and performance direction • Change management, engagement and communication • Self and team capabilities — knowledge, skill and experience level (includes training and coaching) • Team effectiveness, motivation and wellness • New ideas implemented and processes improved	• Vision, business direction and department goals — embraced by team that can articulate them • Case for change well communicated and effectively executed • Recognition given where it is due and performance issues proactively dealt with • Self and all team members achieved development objectives • New ideas & opportunities for improving work methods and processes sought and applied • Created an inclusive positive climate — energized team to achieve better performance than previous year	• Employees want to work on manager's team • The need for change is recognized and championed up through the organization • Sought out as a mentor or coach • Sets the standard for providing regular, on-going feedback • Other managers actively recruit direct reports • Significant number of improvement ideas per team member implemented

Management Results
- Work schedule — people, resources, money and work
- Resource provision and availability (people and tools to do the job)
- Plan implemented
- Progress monitoring, reporting and corrective action

Customer & Relationship Results
- Customer/supplier knowledge, relationships needs and satisfaction
- Service level agreement delivery
- Employee relationships
- Team effectiveness (own and other teams)
- Knowledge sharing and networking within team

- Work and project plans in place to accomplish team objectives
- Put right people in right job at the right time
- Work assigned and work loads balanced
- Control systems & measures in place ensured timely results
- Appropriate resources available at right cost
- A safe work environment is created for all team members
- Built effective working relationship with manager, peers, team members, customers & suppliers
- Full understanding of customer needs gained and applied
- Knowledge-based relationships with other departments/functions, customers/venders drove results
- Proactively built networks to understand big picture and achieve results

- Sets the standard for resource availability, plan delivery and progress monitoring
- On-going planning and control systems achieve results higher than peers and are best practice
- Provides innovating solutions
- Plans and goals fully support other teams
- Networks optimized to achieve exceptional results & create new thinking

Table 7.3 Manager of Others, Specialist

Guiding Principles: (1) Getting results through others. (2) Engaging, training, and serving others. (3) Remove obstacles inhibiting team performance. (4) From teamwork to teambuilding. (5) Taking accountability for success of others. (6) Living and prompting company values. (7) From personal planning to planning for team results. (8) From individual results to providing customer results.

Results	Full Performance	Exceptional Performance
Business, Financial, and Technical Results • Output target achievement e.g., Consulting solutions proposed achieved targeted results, advice & opinions accepted created value —prevented destruction of value • Cost target achievement • Risk target achievement • Quality target achievement • Productivity targets achievement e.g. turnaround time, Project ROI	• Self and team always met targets, due dates and quality standards • Produced consistent results by holding employees to agreed-upon targets, methods and measures • Incremental improvement in results achieved (more with less)	• Targets, due dates and quality standards regularly exceeded • New results in new ways • Set the standard for achievement of delivery results • Productivity efficiency and effectiveness increased significantly each year
Leadership & Growth Results • Goal clarity, alignment and performance direction • Change management, engagement and communication • Team capabilities and skill level (includes training and coaching • Team effectiveness, motivation and wellness • Number of new ideas implemented and processes improved • Personal development and technical skill and knowledge level e.g., new technology	• Vision, business direction and department goals —embraced by team that can articulate them • Creates an inclusive positive climate where team is engaged & energized to achieve better performance than last year • Case for change well communicated and effectively executed • Gives recognition where it is due and proactively deals with performance issues • Self and all team members achieved development objectives • Sought and applied B@$ new ideas & opportunities for improving work methods and processes	• Employees want to work on manager's team • The need for change is recognized and championed up through the organization • Sought out as a mentor or coach • Sets the standard for providing regular, on-going feedback • Team norm is to seek new knowledge and ideas to drive growth • Significant number of improvement ideas per team member implemented

Management Results

- Work schedule — people, resources, money and work
- Resource provision and availability (people and tools to do the job)
- Plan implementation
- Progress monitoring, reporting and corrective action
- Policies and standards compliance, e.g., Quality and risk
- Decision and problem solving quality, e.g.,, build/fix or buy application

- Work and project plans in place to accomplish major team objectives
- Put right people in right job at the right time
- Work assigned and work loads balanced
- Control systems & measures in place ensured timely results and no surprises (data tracking, TQM, problem solving, sales tracking)
- Appropriate resources available at reasonable cost

- On-going planning and control systems achieve results higher than peers' and are best practice
- Other managers actively recruit direct reports

Customer & Relationship Results

- Knowledge of customer/consumer needs
- Customer satisfaction level and customer communication
- Employee relationships (disciplinary and grievances)
- Service level agreement delivery
- Supplier and contractor relationships, agreements and management

- Full understanding of customer needs gained and applied
- Built effective working relationship with boss, peers, team members, customers & suppliers
- Strong external network were available as needed
- Knowledge-based relationships with other departments/ functions, customers / venders used to drive results
- Proactively built networks to understand big picture and achieve results

- Plans and goals fully support other teams and reflect multifunctional thinking
- External networks optimized to introduce new thinking

Results We Don't Want

Just because MOOs represent the first leadership layer doesn't mean that these results are less important than those at higher layers. In fact, you could make the argument that at least in one sense, these results are more important; that if you get it right here, you increase the odds that managers will get it right at higher layers because they have a solid results foundation. If, for instance, someone fails to master basic management skills early on, he will probably be handicapped from a results standpoint since he'll be missing the foundation or building skills that are necessary at higher levels. Additionally, since this layer enables delivery, poor management threatens your ability to serve customers.

Therefore, organizations need to keep a close eye on the type of results MOOs are generating. Inappropriate results should be taken as signs that MOOs are working at the wrong level—generally, the individual contributor level. Some of the key indicators are the following:

Technical/professional results are their primary contribution. When managers persist in doing the work from a previous position or cherry-picking the best work for themselves, they aren't learning to manage. It's fine for MOOs to perform some technical/professional work—as part of teaching or demonstrating, or during emergencies or in response to special problems. When more than one-quarter of the time is spent on doing technical/professional work, however, a problem exists. That MOO isn't learning, and the team is being shortchanged.

Isolation. When managers spend large amounts of time in their office with the door closed or at their computer or out of the office calling on customers, it means they aren't engaging with their people. While isolation, like individual contributor work, may be necessary at times, it's a problem if it's a pattern of behavior. This pattern means they can't or won't engage with other people sufficiently to be an effective MOO. They must learn to engage their team early in their tenure, and if they don't, it's a sign that they're not going to produce results appropriate to this level.

Favoritism. As discussed earlier, caring about all the employees and the enterprise is a needed result. Favoritism means the caring is skewed inappropriately. It also means productivity will eventually suffer since those who aren't favored will not be trying as hard as they could. Managers can also make the mistake of favoring the enterprise at the expense of the team, ensuring that the team is always disadvantaged when any decision or change is made. For instance, they may interpret all organizational rules and processes literally, preventing a team member from acting in a way that produces a better outcome than the "approved" method would; effective MOOs learn to make purposeful exceptions. Conversely, favoring the employee at the expense of the enterprise routinely leads to a lack of connection and will disadvantage the enterprise.

Staff competition. Competing with team members is a carryover from working at the old level. Now the requirement is to engage, support, and teach. Competition is unfair because the MOO has more resources and more information. When Managers of Others capitalize on this advantage to "show people the right way to get this task done," they are abusing their managerial position. When competition is apparent, MOOs need coaching to help them change their identity from team member to team leader.

No Individual Contribution Is Sufficient

Many other signs exist of not making the turn to Manager of Others from Self-Manager. Chapter Ten, "Enabling Layer Transitions," suggests additional indicators that apply here. When the indications materialize, the MOM or a trained HR person should intervene quickly. If new MOOs aren't cut out for managing, the sooner they are moved, the better it is for everyone; moving them quickly can prevent people on that team from being disadvantaged or disillusioned about the enterprise. It may seem useful that the MOO is calling on customers and sales are going up, or is designing the software at a high level of proficiency, but in the long run this individual contributor behavior hurts the enterprise and the employees.

Example

Margo was enthusiastic about tackling the challenges in her new job. She was promoted from Sourcing Associate covering Southern California to Strategic Sourcing Manager for the Asian Region. She inherited a team of ten associates, who had not been delivering needed results. Joe, her new boss, told her to get new contracts as quickly as possible. So, after short meetings with each of her direct reports, she set out to learn the market firsthand and meet key people at the major suppliers. Her team of ten was told to keep doing what they had been doing for the time being.

Because of her deep product knowledge and flair for supplier negotiating, she was a big hit with suppliers. By the end of the first year, Margo had exceeded the delivery targets by 23 percent and added five new suppliers. Her team was now required to do the follow-up work making sure orders were filled and new suppliers were properly enrolled and passed quality inspections. After six more months Margo was 18 percent ahead of her new, bigger target, but the travel was wearing thin. When a key supplier offered her a senior management position running all their Internet business, she jumped at the chance to make more money and dramatically reduce traveling.

Joe was angry because he was back to square one. Despite the increased sourcing, the Asian procurement team was still ineffective, and if he couldn't replace Margo in kind he was sure the delivery would fall off. While there was some improvement, not one member of the procurement team had been developed sufficiently to replace Margo or to drive delivery the way she had. He felt he might have kept her if she had developed her team to do the traveling and negotiating.

Clearly the company was not well served by Margo's approach, but the problem was masked by the improved sourcing results. New Managers of Others can make results improve, but it's only temporary if the appropriate building of capability in others isn't achieved. Something as simple as taking one team member on each sourcing call and over time letting them conduct negotiations would have made a major difference. Joe agreed to make this a requirement in the future. Margo said she knew developing people was important, but only sourcing results were discussed or measured.

8

Self-Managers

Delivering the Products and Services

What results should individual contributors, or Self-Managers, generate? That's a loaded question but an important one; and it's one that often goes unanswered both for the Self-Manager and the Manager of Others. Many Managers of Others assume the Self-Manager population will know what to do if they are given the job description, have an area of specialization, and are provided with general guidance. In fact, many Self-Managers possess only a vague sense of what results they are to produce. Or even worse, they have a mistaken sense of what the required results are, and expend time and energy on the wrong things. I have included this chapter in a book about leaders to help Managers of Others understand what to ask from their people. Also, the Self-Manager population can help itself in the event their manager doesn't help them.

Self-managing employees are the biggest segment of the workforce, and these individuals have titles like salesperson, engineer, analyst, recruiter, dealmaker, lawyer, programmer, stylist, and so on. While they manage tasks, they don't manage people. Sometimes they are asked to head a team of their peers to complete a project, but this is a temporary arrangement, not a permanent part of their job.

A wide range of skills and abilities resides in this layer. Not many businesses require only one skill set from this layer; a diverse set of skills is the norm. In the previous chapter I discussed several populations of self-managing employees and identified some of the management challenges they present. Diversity of skills and abilities is the one constant for this population because there are so many different kinds of work to be done. While diversity can be difficult to manage, a high level of diversity of thought, skills, experience, competence, and approach keeps the enterprise from becoming too predictable to competitors, or too complacent. A wide range of skills produces a wide range of results—it is what helps an enterprise excel in many areas and what gives it its unique character.

The Purpose of the Self-Manager Layer

This layer produces and sells the product or delivers the service. Beyond this central purpose, the layer adds value in other ways. While support positions may not actually touch the product, they enable those that do. In general, the Self-Manager is the least expensive layer, so they help keep the costs of products and services lower than they would be if the leadership layers had hands-on involvement. If managed properly, this layer can produce excellent results, because this is where technical and professional skills reside. By building new technical skills and knowledge, Self-Managers can deliver the product or service in new or better ways. Through collaboration with their peers and with management they can speed up the processes and get synergy. Direct customer contact is a big part of their work; they influence customers' attitudes through the quality of products or services, timely delivery, a positive and helpful attitude, and innovation of all kinds.

This may be obvious to you; I belabor it because the Self-Manager layer is so often subordinated within the greater scheme of things. Individual contributors often receive less training and communication relative to the results expected of them than the layers above them receive. Therefore, I want to emphasize that this layer is ignored at the organization's peril. Its impact on the enterprise is far greater than it might appear. To draw on an earlier analogy, the actors can make or break the movie even with good direction.

Making clear to Self-Managers what is expected, providing the right resources, and giving feedback to help them improve are critical management tasks required to get full value and make the business successful. Flaws in the performance pipeline show up here. If management does its part, then individual contributors are much more likely to do theirs.

(Note: I am focusing in this chapter on individual contributors who have some discretion about (1) how their time is actually spent, (2) how much they interact with peers, and (3) when to challenge what's going on. Hourly workers represented by a bargaining unit are specifically excluded because they are in a different position; an entire book could be written about the issues involved there.)

What the Self-Manager Population Should Deliver

Delivering the product or service is the overarching requirement but doesn't tell the whole story. Individual contributors must also deliver many critical supporting results for this layer to deliver full value. I'm not going to get bogged down in detailing the specific contributions of specialized types of Self-Managers—the technical specifics of how a programmer writes code, or how a dealmaker puts a deal together. Instead, I'm going to focus on the underlying results required for anyone to be successful, results that also help the business and enterprise prosper. These include the following:

- Self-management

- Cooperation

- Customer satisfaction mind-set

- Citizenship

- Learning

- Ideas and innovation

- Influence

- Relationships

Self-Management

Self-management is the foundation of all management, so it is best learned here. It means having the discipline to find out what is needed and the self-control to get it done. Working on what's needed rather than what you feel like working on is the test. Peter Drucker, our greatest management thinker, wrote about management by objectives and self-control. Organizations, however, have embraced management by objectives so enthusiastically that they forget that self-control is equally important. Practicing self-control is much harder than setting goals and tracking performance. It requires several deliberate activities:

1. *Learning what is needed.* Ideally, bosses make it clear to people what is needed, by when, and why. The Performance Pipeline is built on that idea. More likely, bosses spell out some of the work to be done, but not all of it. Individual contributors, therefore, must ask bosses or colleagues what is needed or expected. Sitting around and waiting for instruction costs the company money. Proactive effort is required by everyone (at every level!). If it isn't there, people spend a significant amount of time on secondary, tertiary, or completely irrelevant tasks. People must make it a habit to seek information quickly. This "seeking" approach is especially useful when answers aren't clear or the boss is unavailable.

2. *Planning and time management.* Developing a clear idea of what actions to take, when to take them, and with what resources is fundamental to personal productivity. One key learning from the hundreds of assessments I have done on successful leaders is that the high-achiever plans better than everyone else. At the heart of self-management is time management.

3. *Building the necessary skills.* Many skill-acquisition avenues are available, but the best is coaching from the boss. Being willing to admit, at the earliest stage, that you can't do something important sounds risky. Doing things inappropriately or with mistakes is much riskier. If the boss can't or won't teach, peers are the next best source. Observation, questions, lunchtime conversations (if there is such a thing as lunchtime in your company), and teaming all work. Reaching outside the organization, such as by reading or talking to experts, can be very useful but might not be available. Trial and error can also be a viable learning method. Also, lessons-learned analysis with the boss and with peers is a cheap and practical method. These can be informal but are best done right after an important piece of work is finished or has failed. Go through each step and identify what worked and what didn't.

4. *Asking for feedback.* Learning to seek feedback rather than wait for the boss to initiate it is a valuable skill, since boss-initiated feedback doesn't always take place (for many reasons, including some bosses' reluctance to provide critical or negative feedback). Applying the feedback is critical to success and opens the door for more. Peers have observations to share and may have been on exactly the same learning curve. Asking for peer feedback may provide exactly what is needed and could head off future problems with peers. Being

appreciative and applying the feedback, even if it is painful to do, is important to self-management.

5. *Managing emotions.* When faced with a task or challenge, what is needed is a hard, dispassionate look at what is to be accomplished and what the best way to accomplish it might be. Passion for the task is great, but at this level, people need to learn how to control their emotions to make sure emotions don't get in the way of getting things done. For instance, a Self-Manager may feel angry that he was given what feels like an overly rudimentary job; his resentment makes him carry out the task in a perfunctory, careless manner; the sloppy execution results in a variety of problems requiring costly, time-consuming rework. By learning how to manage emotion, though, people can think about how the enterprise or business normally does the task, what the benefits are to doing it that way, and whether a better (cheaper, faster, higher quality) way might be thought through before deciding what to do. Considerable self-discipline is required. The business or enterprise can't deliver on its brand or its promise to customers if every Self-Manager pursues results based only on his emotions.

6. *Owning their obstacles.* Blaming the obstacles when results aren't forthcoming is a common practice in organizations, but an unacceptable one. Too often, this happens because people don't learn to own their obstacles at the Self-Manager layer. In order to get the results, someone has to "own" the obstacle: assuming accountability for overcoming it, removing it, or getting help to address it. Sometimes a new plan or approach is needed. Sometimes hard work is enough. Whatever the case may be, failure, missed due dates, cost overruns, poor quality, and so on due solely to the presence of an obstacle isn't acceptable. There are always obstacles. It is totally appropriate to expect self-managing

employees to come up with some solutions, not just blame the obstacles or go running to the boss without a recommendation. Applying time more appropriately, learning a new skill, and innovating to overcome obstacles are part of self-management.

7. *Being accountable.* Taking responsibility for delivering assigned work may seem self-evident, but many people come into organizations accustomed to making excuses or blaming others when they don't deliver. Even more commonly, they don't take the time or make the effort to ensure that they can do what they're assigned to do. Making a plan that ensures on-time delivery and applying energy and skill to achieve the plan are routine aspects of self-management. However, the work isn't done until it's correct, completed, connected to other work, and accepted by the customer. Working diligently isn't the same as being accountable. Putting all aspects of the entire task or project together so that the total package is in place is what really counts. Working hard may seem like enough, but it is actually a small portion of what has to be done.

Self-management isn't easy. These activities can be demanding and time consuming. Organizations, however, should recognize the enterprise-sustaining benefits of helping individual contributors master this skill: it can reduce the number of leaders that are needed, improve customer service dramatically, and provide a true source of competitive advantage.

Cooperation

Teamwork is crucial to effective organizational work, but not everything can or should be done by or with a team. Most Self-Managers are likely to spend the majority of their time working individually. For this reason, practicing the art of cooperation is a crucial result at this level. Work seldom goes smoothly, so changes in timing, direction, content, and the like are often required. Cooperation from the Self-Manager population should be automatic when change is needed, when new methods are implemented, when deadlines get moved up, or when projects need to be scaled back. Individual contributors need to change their methods, stay late, give up a pet project, share their resources and skills with other functions, and so on. If they don't cooperate in these ways, productivity suffers. Uncooperative people force their bosses to waste time and energy on persuasion, coaxing, or reprimanding. And when one person doesn't cooperate, it often encourages a colleague to follow suit. Everything slows down and gets harder right when speed and productivity are needed most. Cooperative people adjust and move on; uncooperative people slow down and resist.

Customer Satisfaction Mind-set

Most Self-Managers do not see the actual customer, but everyone serves customers. Recruiters in Human Resources can recruit people with good customer skills and a service mind-set. Finance can do analyses of costs to help keep costs down so the customer can ultimately be offered a better price. Engineers can design products that are easy for customers to use and maintain. Supply chain people can schedule convenient delivery dates and times.

I should note here that this result does not and should not include "internal customers." Having internal customers—that is, one function serving another function—sets up the wrong measurement and creates an internal relationship that hurts teamwork. For instance, "We in manufacturing are your customer, HR, so you better get us the programs we want." Everything Manufacturing does, such as product quality, delivery, and cost management, should benefit the paying customer. HR can and should work with Manufacturing to help add customer value, not just manufacturing value, in the programs they design and deliver.

Here's the results-oriented mind-set Self-Managers should develop: Start with the paying customer and draw a line back to their desks. That line may go directly to them if they are in Sales or Service, but it may also go through Sales or through Manufacturing or through Engineering before it gets to their desks. With this understanding, their thinking and acting can be done with customer satisfaction in mind.

Citizenship

An enterprise is a community in the sense that it has goals and needs that affect everyone, has a code of conduct or rules for everyone to follow, and succeeds or fails on the basis of this combined effort. Self-Managers are the largest segment of that community, so they have a major impact on what kind of community it is. Visions, slogans, and the like don't mean anything if they aren't pursued or honored by this large segment. Some of the worst service I have ever received has been delivered (or not delivered) by people wearing a "Total Quality" button; in another case, bad service was provided by representatives standing under a banner that read, "Our Customers Come First."

Performing assigned tasks, staying out of trouble, and being polite to the boss aren't enough. What individual contributors need to learn is an innate sense of doing the right thing for the good of the company. It's not just about behaving when everyone is watching them. Instead, it means volunteering for a difficult task, or speaking up when a colleague is unfairly negative about the enterprise. Self-Managers must also learn to make sure that work meets standards, plans are aligned with strategy, and mission-critical work gets done first. We can and should expect every Self-Manager to internalize the vision, mission, and values so they will work and behave appropriately—whether they're at work or out in the community. Citizenship is a broad term with broad responsibilities—from trying to do one's best on any task to, when interacting with outsiders, being supportive of what the enterprise and business are trying to do.

Learning

You may never have thought of learning within the framework of results, but it's essential for performance at this level. Most of the enterprise's technical, professional, and operational know-how sits with the Self-Manager population. Many of them were hired for their knowledge, training, or skills, and senior members have years of experience and expertise. This collective capability is an asset to the enterprise that must be nurtured and enhanced. Keeping the collective capability current with evolving technologies of all kinds is a key business requirement. Other layers do the exploration of the state of the art and the investment in new technology, but the Self-Manager population has to learn and apply. They may need to change how they work in order to utilize new technology and new learnings, for instance.

They also have to learn about customer needs, competitive practices, and market conditions. Adjusting to changes in customer needs or market conditions requires good self-management coupled with this learning in order to produce the right results. Business strategy changes as a result of these changing conditions, and the Self-Manager population must keep up.

Individual contributors must also gain knowledge about environmental conditions, economic trends, and social or societal changes. External factors that affect the enterprise and the business also affect the Self-Manager population in one way or another.

Ideas and Innovations

Ideas and innovations keep the enterprise or business from becoming obsolete. They provide new solutions to customers' problems; they gain or sustain competitive advantage; and they lower costs or improve quality. The largest segment of the workforce—the Self-Manager population—should be the biggest contributors of ideas and innovations. They have the technical and professional skills; they meet the customer; and they often have fresh perspectives, as many of them are relatively new to the company. Because some individual contributors may be reluctant to contribute their ideas or are uncertain about how to contribute them, bosses need to make this expectation clear.

The highest-paid engineers, scientists, accountants, and other professionals are usually expected to innovate. People who are new to the company or in entry-level positions, however, may feel as if they lack the credibility or power base to suggest an idea, especially one that is different or entails some risk. Yet these individuals have the least interest in preserving the status quo, and they are looking to make their mark in the enterprise. These two factors, combined with their fresh perspective, technical expertise, and numbers (large percentage of employee population) mean that they should be encouraged to be creative in their work. The challenge for many companies is learning how to encourage them and not suppress their ideas in the name of conformity and compliance.

Influence

Even though this population doesn't have direct responsibility for other people (by definition), they are often in a position to cause change or to move their peers in a new and better direction. By combining the kind of results I have discussed so far, they can know what's needed or what can be improved. If they don't have any influence, the enterprise or the business loses that potential value.

Influence means that their ideas will get heard and action is likely to follow. Their opinion is sought on matters of importance, and their ideas tend to prevail when a discussion takes place. If they are thorough and reasoned in their thinking, if their learning and application are consistently effective, and if they have a positive outlook, then they can have influence with their peers and their boss. Thus, they must understand that they will be given every opportunity to be influential and that they should take the time and put in the work necessary to be employees of influence.

Relationships

This last underlying result is absolutely essential for success at this level, yet it's frequently ignored—few Self-Managers are held accountable for building strong relationships. Like our earlier result, cooperation, this one involves a people skill. Yet it is a broader result than cooperation, requiring the ability to build and maintain a diversity of business relationships. It doesn't involve just accommodating others but learning to work productively and creatively with a range of individuals.

Causing others to have a positive opinion about you is the goal, and it takes effort and a willingness to listen and support them. Some kinds of good opinions are not of much value to the business; for example, "She is really funny" or "He always listens to my problems." What matters most is the working relationship. Social relationships make life more enjoyable, but working relationships make work more successful. People should want to work with each other rather than "have to" collaborate. Requiring the Self-Manager population to develop good working relationships with everyone should be explicitly stated and not left to chance.

The Whole Job

With all the variety that resides in this layer, defining the whole job is challenging. Table 8.1 is a good example of how it can be done. Required work values have been spelled out to provide a framework for thinking about what is expected and to establish the proper mind-set on results like citizenship and innovation. The work values also clarify the management relationship, communicating that it should be a proactive one in which the individual contributor keeps the boss informed. Adopting these work values means the Self-Manager will accept the critical job requirements.

The company that built the performance standards displayed in Table 8.1 was trying to make some critical strategic changes. They had launched a major improvement program, and these performance standards conveyed the breadth of results required of everyone. Asterisked items were of particular significance to those strategic changes and helped each layer see in specific terms what its contribution should be.

Self-Management Results and Leadership Results categories demonstrate how this company communicates and commits to full utilization of each Self-Manager's capability. The expectations for applying personal discipline and personal improvement are spelled out.

These expectations also must be measured; clear standards for exceptional performance is particularly important for this population. New college graduates and other new entrants to the company often desire a career, not just a job. Desires to "get ahead," do more challenging work, make a bigger contribution, and earn more money or other rewards are normal. Defining the requirements for exceptional performance helps everyone understand what it takes to be considered a person of high potential or a fast-tracker. Providing specific targets for exceptional performance helps focus effort on results that matter rather than on secondary or inconsequential objectives. Not everyone wants a bigger challenge, but those that do benefit greatly from clear definitions.

Rather than have the boss define all the unacceptable effort or activities, this company chose to make some of it explicit in the performance standards document. Defining things in this way helps with self-management and provides boundaries that are easy to understand. These "Indicators of Need to Develop in Place"

Table 8.1 Performance Standards, Self-Manager

Required Work Values

- Adopting enterprise's values and culture
- Meeting industry professional standards
- Proactively finding new and better ways to accomplish the work*
- Connecting management to the work challenges
- Identifying problems early and seeking solutions

Performance Dimensions	Full Performance	Exceptional Performance	Indicators of Need to Develop in Place
Operational/Technical/Financial Results Individual or project/program results • Cost targets • *Individual or project/program goals and due dates* • *Work orders* • *Sales, customer influence* • *Accuracy, timeliness of analysis*	• Sale/Project/Process costs within budget* • All delivery targets and due dates met • Professional standards met in all regards • Work accomplished according to safety and quality guidelines and practices	• All targets and due dates exceeded • Quality of work is model for peers • Ideas to improve work processes add extra value*	• Not on track to meet due dates, not catching up • Safety or quality violation • Wastes resources* • Doesn't know the standards
Self Management • *Plans and organization of work* • *Cost, quality and timeliness* • *Effective use of resources* • *Success of unit* • *Measures and controls*	• Personal work plans assure on-time delivery • Personal work plans fit with others in/outside of the Unit • Obstacles owned and overcome* • Early problem detection misses	• Personal time management resulted in a significant productive increase* • Process improvements in own and other's work increased Unit's results* • Personal growth set the standard for the team.	• Excessive socializing • Lacks focus and/or commitment • Sense of closure comes too early • Stops and starts

Competency	Examples		Ineffective Behaviors
Leadership • *Influence* • *Individual development* • *Teamwork/team play* • *Values/Ethics*	• Right information provided to right people, in right way, at right time • Team play contributed to team success • Personal behavior consistent with Enterprise values/ethics • Self-development led to support for program/process changes*	• Influence skills led to peer acceptance for needed change • Increased productivity through new process creation*	• Can't sell his/her ideas • Insufficient communication effort • Resists change • Doesn't live the values
Relationships • *Customer/contractor relations* • *Collaborate with peers, other functions and business units* • *Support the boss and team* • *Networking*	• Effective working relationship with boss and coworkers created synergy • "How can I help you?" and "How am I hindering?" regularly asked • Network with peers and other key parties (e.g., customer) gets things done • Success of the team and organization always placed ahead of personal ambition*	• Model for effective working relationships with peers • Gets needed results through external networks* • Routinely helped peers in/outside function succeed	• Keeps to him/herself • Not responsive to needs or requests of peers* • Ignores boss, doesn't prepare for meetings with boss • Puts self ahead of team
Customer/Patient/User • *Product safety and efficacy* • *Knowledge of customer needs/expectations* • *Feedback to Enterprise/boss*	• Met commitments to customer value creation • Customer feedback influence product and process improvement* • Safety protocols strictly followed	• Sought by others for customer knowledge, trends and understanding of customer needs (segmentation, buying patterns)* • Quality of customer feedback redirected programs and plans	• Unaware of customer issues • Doesn't understand quality or safety standards • Not relating with customers

*Critical to new strategic initiative.

(column four) help companies make improvements at every layer in how they operate, and break out of bad habits acquired by their leaders.

Results We Don't Want

The "indicators of need to develop in place" also suggest attitudes and actions that are counterproductive. Beyond the specifics of each column, they indicate the following three harmful traits Self-Managers often manifest:

Cynicism destroys trust and confidence. When employees become cynical, they don't respond properly to key management requests or enterprise programs. "This won't work" and "He doesn't know what he is doing" are the language of the cynic. You can hear it as you leave meetings or after major presentations. Self-Managers should express legitimate concerns; they need to talk about specific actions rather than display their attitude. Cynicism is catching, so bosses need to address it early so that it doesn't spiral into the next counterproductive trait.

Resistance to change or to anything new is easier to spot than cynicism and just as troublesome. Resistance shows up in a variety of ways: passive resistance (not saying no, but never saying yes), slowing down, giving less than full effort, and prolonging arguments. People do resist for legitimate reasons, and they should be allowed to put forth their points of view, but after a decision has been made, resistance must end.

Narcissism seems to be more prevalent now than ever before. Narcissism is expressed in "it's all about me" language: "I am happy to talk to you as long as we talk about me." Narcissists aren't team players unless the purpose of the team is to make them successful; they have big ideas and bold plans, but these have little to do with the boss's or business's goals. These people fail to support peers, give time and energy to achieve team goals, and work effectively on teams.

Enabling Exceptional Performance: The Technical Performance Pipeline

In most companies, professionals, engineers, scientists, relationship managers, and other individual contributors exist who deliver exceptional results but don't want to be a manager. When they bump up against the job ceiling—they are holding the best technical/professional position available to them—they become restless. They would like to do more and earn more, but no options exist to do so, and they don't want to work harder for the same pay. Consequently, these people complain to colleagues and bosses; they lose commitment and their performance suffers; and they may look for and find other jobs.

The solution, though, is not to make these exceptional performers managers when they clearly prefer to stay in their Self-Manager roles. Nonetheless, companies reflexively offer disaffected high-performers management jobs to keep them with the company. Sometimes Self-Managers turn these offers down, and sometimes they grudgingly accept them in order to gain more money, authority, and challenges. While a minority may become excellent managers as they shift their work values appropriately (to the next management layer), most of them continue to do the technical/professional work for which they were trained and where they were successful. Excellent Self-Managers can become average to poor managers.

This scenario exists in almost every company I have worked with. The Leadership Pipeline becomes clogged at the bottom. The Performance Pipeline isn't delivered. If you're facing this scenario, the best course of action is to build a Technical Performance Pipeline. By creating a series of more challenging and broader-scope positions, you offer a valuable alternative for advancement rather than losing highly capable technical and professional people to another company or creating a manager who doesn't want to manage.

The Technical Performance Pipeline (TPP) is a series of increasingly more responsible Self-Manager positions that impact the effectiveness or direction of the function, business, or enterprise. By tackling the biggest technical/professional challenges, they add unique value. To see how the TPP looks for a big company, see Figure 8.1.

The TPP helps advance the function's, business's, or enterprise's understanding of the technical playing field, brings new technology into the organization, and influences the strategic

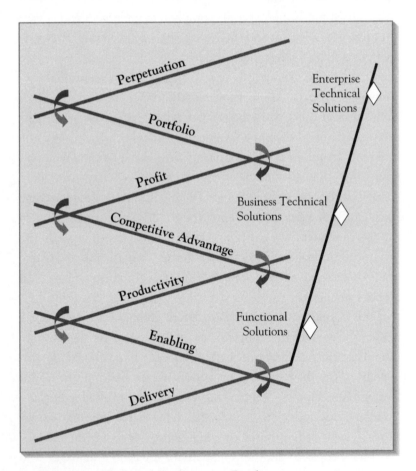

Figure 8.1 Technical Performance Pipeline

direction. Managing the use of specific technology across the enterprise is a common requirement.

At first glance, the TPP may strike you as similar to the Technical Career Ladder. The latter provides higher-level positions, usually for engineers and scientists, that help the function and possibly the business address difficult technical challenges. Technical career ladders help retain top technical talent by creating a definable career path.

The Technical Performance Pipeline, however, is different from the Technical Career Ladder in three significant ways. First, the TPP is intended to drive Business Results, not technical results. Second, the TPP enables the organization to teach others and take responsibility for how some specific technology is used across the enterprise. Third, and perhaps most important, the intent of the Technical Performance Pipeline is different from that of the Ladder. The TPP is intended to improve the business, while the Technical Career Ladder is used to help functional technology but primarily to help the person. Technical performance pipeline members attend the staff meetings of the entity they service; technical career ladder people attend their boss's staff meetings.

Benefits of a Technical Performance Pipeline

Just about every organization should have a TPP, especially if it's struggling with Managers of Others who don't manage—who reflexively return to the technical work they love and who find it difficult if not impossible to transition to managerial work values. It's also crucial if the company is losing its Self-Managers to other companies or if these people are losing their drive. Creating this variation on the Performance Pipeline is relatively easy to do, and the small investment in time is rewarded with a range of benefits:

- Technical expertise can be leveraged to solve tough business problems if highly proficient technical people understand the business. That is one reason they should attend the function, business, or enterprise staff meetings.

- Knowledge is managed more actively. The higher-level technical expert has responsibility for knowledge transfer to individuals and other businesses in the enterprise.

- Higher-level talent can be attracted or retained. Technical/professional stars who work for other companies but feel that their career is blocked find the Technical Performance Pipeline attractive. People want to have the challenge of another rung on the ladder to climb, and the TPP offers that challenge.

- Strategy at the function, business, and enterprise level is better informed by better technical information. In fact, the strategic direction in companies with technical products depends on a proper understanding of what technology can deliver now or will deliver in the foreseeable future.

- Product or service innovation resulting from technical advancement is a likely source of competitive advantage.

- Managers can concentrate on managing people, money, customers, and the future because their technology is being managed separately but with the function, business, or enterprise in mind.

- The TPP is free. No new people have to be added. Managers who are strong technically but poor as managers can be shifted effectively using the Technical Performance Pipeline. Fewer,

better managers will deliver the same or better
results.

Some organizations find that they lack the people to do the
jobs the Technical Performance Pipeline identifies, so they may
need to add a few people on the basis of what it reveals. If the
selections are done correctly, they will add great value.

Defining the Technical Performance Pipeline

The expected results spelled out earlier in the chapter also apply
to everyone on the technical performance pipeline. Going beyond
those expected results is the difference. Making additional required
results explicit and relevant to your function, business, or company
takes some thought. It helps to think of it in this way:

Level	Additional Results Expected
Enterprise level	• Technical strategic direction for enterprise • Applied technology meeting highest standards across the enterprise • Globally recognized expert • Recommendations for acquisition
Business level	• Technical information for business strategy • Business team membership • Uniformity of technology application across the business • Technical solutions for business problem • Team member for acquisition deal
Function level	• Knowledge transfer through coaching • Technical project leadership • Technical solutions to increase functional competitive advantage • New product ideas • Mentor relationships

You may need to add to or modify these suggested additional results. Business-specific challenges should dictate your list. Whatever your list turns out to be, *it should help technical people learn to think at the layer they serve.* Choose these people carefully; don't force them into the jobs. It is entirely possible that you don't have anyone for the very top job or that no one who is now managing would rather move back into a position specified by the TPP. Getting the results is the objective, not making promotions for engineers.

Table 8.2 is an example of how one company created a technical performance pipeline simply and effectively. This company had been a technical leader in its industry, but through lack of attention and failure to hire new college graduates during an industry downturn it had lost its leadership position. Their technical performance pipeline became the guide for external recruiting, as they used it for developing position and candidate specifications. Communication of the position requirements and of their intent to rebuild was easier and clearer with a TPP. Discussions with candidates focused on expected business impact and required mind-set, not just technical contributions. While recruiting was difficult because the company was going after high-level technical people, obtaining acceptances to offers extended was easy—the TPP helped the company make offers that ambitious technical/professionals couldn't refuse.

Table 8.2 Technical Path Levels

Level and Performance Contribution	Description	Key Shift in Results Expected
Consulting Technical Advisor *Building Technical Capability in the Organization*	• Fully skilled technical specialist. Spends 80–90% of time doing technical work and 10–20% mentoring others • Consults globally on technical problems, shares experiences and trains and develops others	• Applied specific technical knowledge and provided key data, expertise, and advice to support decision making
Principal Technical Expert *Creating Competitive Advantage*	• Establishes the framework for technical excellence • Ensures best practices are understood and followed • Sets technical direction and informs operating plan by identifying the right research and technical areas of focus • Informs the business strategy and comes up with solutions to complex technical and business problems	• Managed research and developed technical methods and standards for area of expertise in support of achieving project, regional, or corporate plans and strategy
Leading Technical Expert *Changing the Way the Industry Does Business*	• Sits at the headquarter site and will always influence industry and corporate strategy • Develops a process, technique, or concept that has a significant impact to the industry and enterprise's ability to achieve strategic plans • This person is usually a visionary and is a leader in international forums	• Set technical strategy focusing on ongoing identification of new strategies and targets • Creates strategic opportunity for [company] that would not be possible without industry changing technical contribution

Part III

Successful Implementation of the Performance Pipeline

9

Creating a Context for Performance

The Performance Pipeline, no matter how thoughtfully the model has been crafted, doesn't succeed by itself. It exists in a "context," and that context affects every single employee's results and the overall success of the company. To help you understand what "context" refers to, I'd like to use the analogy of farming. This analogy may strike you as strange, but bear with me; it will help you grasp how to use the pipeline effectively given your organization's particular context.

Think of context as the soil in which your people are planted. It nourishes some kinds of performance, say great service or timely performance feedback, while at the same time inhibiting other kinds of performance, such as speed of response to customers or innovation.

If context is the soil and all employees (seeds!) are planted in that soil, then it follows that a leader's role is that of farmer. Leaders are both seeds (to their boss) and farmers (for their own people). Leaders should make a farmer's contribution: select the right seeds, plant them properly, analyze the soil and—on the basis of the results of the analysis—enrich it, remove the rocks and weeds (obstacles), and take the weather into account. As of this writing, at least, the weather (business climate) isn't favorable.

As pointed out in the Introduction, we are in a period of great uncertainty. Farmers need to be very active or risk losing their crops. Tending to your soil also includes removing things that inhibit seed growth. In particular, weeds and other vegetation that use up the nutrients must be removed. Adding nutrients like the

Performance Pipeline makes it more likely that the seeds (people) will produce the best crop (adding value for customers).

The point is that you can't expect the performance pipeline to do all the work for you. The more you're aware of and acting upon the contextual factors, the better the performance pipeline will function and the better your company will perform.

Test Yourself

How your company responds to the following simple situations will tell you quite a bit about your context for performance:

- You have an idea. Are you more likely to be encouraged to pursue it or told it won't work here?

- You need an important decision made quickly to close a deal. Are you expected to make it yourself after consultation, or is it expected that you will pass it up to the highest levels?

- You have missed your budget. Will you wonder if anyone cares, or will you expect to be punished in some way?

- You are aware of a problem in your area. Are you expected to tell your boss the whole story right away, or make the situation sound better than it is, or delay communication, hoping the problem will work itself out?

Obviously, many other self-diagnostic questions exist. Your answers make clear the context in which you work. You have to decide if the context you have enables your leaders to deliver the required results—this is absolutely essential for the business to perform as intended. Knowing whether or not the soil supports required crop growth is a major requirement for any farmer!

How Your Context Is Defined

The business context in your company or business is determined by a wide range of requirements. You probably inherited some requirements that are hard to change; for instance, your founders established requirements many years ago, and they're ingrained in the culture—things like their original vision, mission, and values define the culture and direct performance. Most requirements, however, come from choices you or your bosses have made, such as the operating model you chose and are currently using (and probably haven't thought about enough). Operating models define how decisions are made, what processes will be used, what standards will be employed, and where certain kinds of work will be done. The business context is reinforced by management practices you chose, such as how you are organized, the kind of people you recruit, the goal-setting systems you have put in place, the development processes being used, the way performance is judged and recognized, and what you do with poor performers. Every leader is affected by all of these variables. Context, therefore, is more than culture and is rarely neutral. It is either helping or hurting, and you need to know which requirements help and which hurt.

For your performance pipeline to be effective, you may have to change some or even all of these requirements. This step is necessary to support the new performance you are after or to succeed in this new business environment. Changing any requirements, however, can be a challenge. A strong commitment to a clearly defined "change requirement" is needed. Challenges of this sort are not for the fainthearted because there always seems to be a large, vocal group of people dedicated to preserving the status quo. Also, many requirements are often implicit, making it difficult to surface them for purposes of discussion and change. Be aware that veteran and highly influential executives are often those most resistant to changing these contextual requirements; and that this resistance can be either open or more subtle (such as passive-aggressive behaviors). To deal with this, make sure you understand what specific changes must be made, and communicate them clearly and frequently. This strategy might not melt all the resistance, but it will help you make the strongest case possible for doing so.

I'm stressing the importance of changing requirements because some companies have been overly dependent on the Performance Pipeline to drive all the needed performance. From a performance standpoint, though, context is critical. More specifically, three types of context changes are often necessary for most companies: cultural elements that are mismatched with strategic plans; operating models that are too small to allow for needed growth or too small for the size of the business; and organization design including the distribution of authority that doesn't go down far enough. Let's examine some likely changes more closely.

Cultural Requirements

Culture usually comprises several elements, not just one, that were relevant to success at some point in the past. Going back to our earlier farming analogy, think about elements of culture as the roots of a tree. The roots usually aren't visible, but they exert tremendous influence on the health and strength of the tree. When these roots were embedded, they were a force for driving good performance. As companies and businesses evolve, some of those roots hinder progress. Having the roots mismatched with business requirements makes it tough to succeed. Consider this example:

Example
Through effective strategic analysis, a major trucking company decided to focus more on logistics. This company had grown rapidly through many acquisitions over a

short period of time. It made money through its assets—for example, truck leasing and renting, with or without drivers; truck stops; maintenance facilities; and the like. Knowing the assets—how many it had, where they were, what condition they were in—was critically important. Truck drivers face all the risks associated with over-the-road travel, so knowing and following all the appropriate truck maintenance requirements and obeying the highway safety requirements were important. Trucking is capital-intensive, so to succeed, the company had to monitor the returns on existing assets and recognize when to invest in new ones.

Logistics, on the other hand, is a different kind of business. It involves all the elements surrounding the collection, transportation, storage, and delivery of components or products, often requiring government inspection or customs clearance. Packing and repacking are sometimes part of it. Finding the best set of choices for transporting inbound components and materials to manufacturers and then moving finished goods to customers or consumers is the core requirement. Significant learning of what the choices are, who the right partners might be for today's project or the longer term, and how best to stay informed on the location of goods being moved are key challenges. This company also had to respond to evolving customer needs, such as doing business in additional countries, and to customer service expectations that were escalating. Many new kinds of work were required, and the way this work got accomplished was quite different from traditional trucking. Learning was now critical.

As you might imagine, this company's leaders struggled with the new requirements for logistics work. Close examination of how the leaders performed led to the conclusion that culturally they were "knowers" and not "learners."

Root	**Observed Practices**	**Underlying Values**
Knowing	*Avoid mistakes*	*Know the company*
	Learn more and more about a very small universe, the assets	*Experience in Operations*
	Using checklists	*Control*

The practices and values required for "learning" are quite different:

Root	**Typical Practices**	**Underlying Values**
Learning	*Learn from mistakes*	*New ideas*
	Change readily to a better approach	*Continuous improvement*
	Conduct research	*Best practice and new methods*

The new root or requirement is learning with some knowing; this represented a significant change from the previous all-knowing requirement. This meant that fresh learning requirements had to be embedded in each leader's job. As you can see from the charts, leaders had to be measured on how they learned from mistakes and made changes and improvements rather than clinging to old practices and avoiding any risk taking. Logistics challenges have many venues, not just the highway. Without this type of shift in culture, the performance pipeline would never achieve its performance potential for the now logistics-focused company.

Similarly, another cultural shift was from a family root to a team root. In the past, the trucking company's context involved a strong focus on family and family values. The CEO emphasized the importance of loyalty and commitment, and in turn, employees reflexively depended on the paternal CEO for guidance: "What does [the CEO] think?" was always a question people asked themselves and others.

As the logistics strategy was implemented, many new people were added to fill the new kinds of jobs that had been created. New skills and experience were needed to pull off the transition to logistics, but hiring wasn't going well. External candidates sensed the mismatch between their needs and the company's environment. Businesses and functions were asked to nominate candidates for these new jobs but wouldn't do it. So, a thorough analysis was conducted. It became clear that "family" had some inhibiting contextual elements.

Root	**Observed Practices**	**Underlying Values**
Family	*Recruit clones*	*People who are like us*
	Hire from within	*Loyalty*
	Outsiders must be experts	*Barriers to entry*
	New people proceed with caution	*Protection of members*
	"Father Knows Best"	*Whatever the CEO wants*

A different context was needed to staff the logistics-oriented company properly. A "team"-based approach was adopted:

Root	Typical Practices	Underlying Values
Team	Recruit those who have the most to offer	Talent
	Reward team performance as well as individual results	Winning
	Get rid of poor performers	High-performers
	Keep all members informed	Cooperation

"Family" is an exclusionary idea, in that if you aren't born into the family or don't get "adopted," you can't be a member. "Family" and "knowing" together are extremely exclusionary. Family is constrained by the belief that "father [the CEO] knows best." All major decisions flow up to the CEO. Families can fight all day and get nothing done, but at the end of the day they are still a family. "Team" requires the ability to perform, so those who can perform are welcome. If team members fight with each other all day and get nothing done, they soon disappear.

Thus, the company introduced team-based measurements, with a broad range of targets. Team play became one criterion for selection and a regular discussion item on the CEO's meeting agenda. This didn't mean discarding all aspects of the company's family-focused culture but integrating its best features with the new team requirements. The organization continued to prize values such as loyalty and caring, but not to the point that underperformers were given a free pass.

As a result of this contextual shift and its use of the performance pipeline, this company has reached the number *one rating from customers for third-party logistics in the United States.*

Other Cultural Elements

The shifts in cultural requirements that organizations must make can run the gamut, but it's useful to familiarize yourself with some of the more common ones. Here are two that I've found have been emerging in recent years and that can have a profound impact on performance.

Retailers and newspapers traditionally have had a *short-term orientation, but many environmental factors necessitate training leaders to possess a long-term perspective as well.* Season-to-season thinking, for instance, is particularly noticeable in clothing retailers. Long-term thinking is driven out by the frenzied pursuit of next season's styles and the sell-off of this season's surplus or unwanted styles or colors. Manufacturing cycles, with the work usually done in a different country, encourage annual thinking; the strategic cycle would be one quarter otherwise. Some retailers have argued with me that fashion and styles aren't predictable, so why invest in long-term thinking and planning?

Yet brand identity, sourcing, partnerships, people, facilities (stores), information technology, and capital all require long-term thinking and planning, and these factors have had an increasing impact on performance in the retailing segment. Clothing retailers are constantly looking for CEOs outside their company, in part because of their failure to do the long-term planning necessary to develop their own people for the position. Overexpansion is also a common problem as retailers respond to the demands of the moment rather than assess the demand curve over time. Clearly, long-term thinking and planning would make a difference for leaders at higher levels. Going back to the Performance Pipeline levels, therefore, long-term thinking would be a new results requirement for senior-level executives, and short-term thinking would remain a requirement for Managers of Others and Self-Manager populations.

Root	Observed Practices	Underlying Values
Short term	Short-term thinking	Today's results
	Endless hard work	Effort
	Highly focused on the here and now	Get it done

Root	Typical Practices	Underlying Values
Long term and short term	Frequent strategic-thinking events	Sustaining competitive advantage
	Relationship-building	Lasting partnerships
	Developing leaders	Business continuity
	Robust capital allocation process	Long-term success

One of the most pervasive cultural shifts needed involves *transactional versus systems thinking*. Financial service companies exhibit transactional thinking at great expense to themselves and great annoyance to their customers. In today's market, systems thinking would deliver much greater customer satisfaction and lower costs. It makes no sense these days to incur marketing costs for things like credit card solicitations, often preapproved, to people who already have cards with that bank or firm, or to people who can't afford them.

If there were a systems view of customers—what are all the things we know or can know about customers—financial services results would be much less volatile and cost would eventually be much lower. Transactional thinking looks at pieces, and systems thinking looks at the whole, at how pieces are connected and how they affect each other.

Root	Observed Practices	Underlying Values
Transactions	Short-term thinking	New accounts
	Focused on my organization	Meeting my goals
	Plans not integrated	Winning individually
	Conflict at every interface	My success

Root	Typical Practices	Underlying Values
Systems	Looking for connections	Systems thinking
	Using the whole organization	Our success
	Building a product continuum	New customers and customer retention

Again, I'm not suggesting that transactional thinking should be eliminated as one of the results leaders should strive for and be measured on. It's just that it isn't enough. As the world gets smaller, as new entrants drive competition, and as world events impact every business, no company can afford to have transactional-only thinkers in leadership positions.

At this point, you may be reflecting on the culture change programs your company has launched. Isn't this change effort sufficient to create a new context and shift the requirements at all leadership levels? Unfortunately, the answer is no. Banners, slogans, posters, and speeches don't cause fundamental change. While understanding the need for change and being clear about what must change are useful, individual accountability for producing new results in new ways is the key driver. The Performance Pipeline allows you to quickly change individual accountability. Changing the culture is more likely if there is a performance pipeline to distribute the accountability for new results associated with the change and to set new standards. Keep this symbiotic relationship between results and change in mind, and never forget that this relationship is what produces great performance.

Operating Model

Start-ups, small companies, and even larger, tradition-bound enterprises often operate with a founder-based or paternalistic model. In order to stay in business, most decisions are made by the owner or founder. It's their money, their idea, and their reputation. Hanging on to this model as long as possible is the norm. Meetings are called when the owner or paternalistic CEO wants them; this type of leader dictates the agenda and the discussion. People around the CEO are usually operationally oriented; they are there to complete tasks. Only when the evidence is compelling do these CEOs consider letting go or delegating (opening additional facilities that require on-site management is one obvious example of the need to delegate). Vision, mission, and values are their foundation for defining success, so they expound on them frequently. For these types of leaders, getting everyone to sign up for the company and its beliefs is a high priority. Successors often adopt the same management style.

If the company succeeds and grows, this initial "operating model" starts to pinch. Speed that came from having a decisive owner-leader turns into waiting in line for time with the overworked big boss. New hires don't get the same indoctrination from this harried leader on vision, mission, and values. More discipline and better processes are needed to handle all this and keep the business profitable. In other words, these companies need a new and different operating model.

Example

Company C had been a small regional service provider in the Midwest. On the basis of the founder's unusually clear and compelling idea, Company C boldly entered a difficult industry. In the early years it fought for survival without much financial cushion. Experts were engaged to deliver the service while the founder managed the business side. The business was run on a day-to-day basis, and problems were addressed as they came up. The first ten years were difficult, but acceptance started to take hold in the marketplace. Contracts were won; satisfied users multiplied and spread the word about the company's success; and new services were added.

Business growth required some additional executives to help lead major functions and share the business's decision making. Instead of the owner making all decisions, a small team, the Office of the Chairman, discussed options and made the tough decisions. The owner, now titled "Chairman," was still final decision maker on many critical items.

As business grew, new facilities were built or acquired. Company C became a major business with national advertising and a national customer base. Several thousand employees were on the payroll. Revenues pushed past $1 billion. Decisions came fast and furiously. New executives felt the need to install processes like strategic planning, and senior management held monthly meetings. These efforts had mixed results because participants weren't convinced that they were things the owner wanted.

This operating model produced excessive workloads and frustration with the rate of progress. Function leaders refused to work together. Conflicts between operating facilities emerged regarding product offerings, processes to be followed, and assignment of users; these conflicts weren't managed or resolved. Company C had outgrown its operating model.

Changing the CEO or changing key leaders won't fix this situation. It isn't a person problem; it's a context problem. The operating model doesn't fit the current reality. A new operating model that lets decisions be made at the right level with the right speed is needed. A more disciplined approach for adding new products and services is needed to ensure that all users receive the same level of service. More strategic *planning to map the future and how to achieve it, more leadership development to embed appropriate leadership capability, and greater organizational learning are all important new requirements.*

To convey the needed changes, the CEO and Chairman agreed to a major change in the operating model (Table 9.1). The "soil" had to be enriched so that customer value could be delivered consistently and at the right cost. Company C made significant changes to product quality routines, leadership development, and strategic planning to make sure every user at whatever facility they chose got the same service at the right standard.

Company C defined both the new present and the likely future to communicate the viability of this new model to all leaders. They had to convey that moving a little bit toward today wasn't going to be good enough. Every leader had to know that much more change was coming but that it would come in manageable steps.

Organization Design

Organization choices need to be reexamined regularly. As businesses evolve and grow new structures, so too are revised job designs, better processes, and a reallocation of authority usually needed. Some examples of needed changes in organization that I have encountered will make issues clear.

From Bureaucracy to Ownership

Business columnists and other pundits tell us that management is a dying concept and it is time for something new. Certainly bad management practices abound, but that doesn't mean the end of management. Ideally, it means the end of "bad management"—a pejorative label that usually applies to bureaucratic management. When constructing your performance pipeline, you need to keep

Table 9.1 Company C

	Past	Today	Future
	Small Company Model "A few good people" From Start-up to Now	**Bigger Business Model Focused on Excellence** "A great team" From Now to Five Years Out	**World Leader Model** "World's best practice" Beyond Five Years
Direction	• Visionary leaders — Visionary Product Concept	• Clarity of direction and identity -strategically managed and customer focused	• One company — teamwork and leading-edge practices
Culture	• Knowing culture with high loyalty and strong family orientation	• Learning culture with high accountability	• Cultural renewal driven by business and environmental realities
Leadership	• Strong company values and a commitment to leadership • Closely held strategy and decision making	• Clear definition of "The [Company] Leader" — business and talent mindset is key, becoming the best place to work • Transparent, honest and direct relationships — customers, Board, employees, suppliers	• Anticipates and defines its future • The best leaders and the best place to work
Management Model	• Operationally oriented, short-term focus • Insufficient process discipline and accountability; no single identity	• New management model to drive process discipline, teamwork and speed • Innovative and collaborative work environment • Consistency of service, brand, leadership	• Entrepreneurship at every level • World leader in innovation and user-centered services • Evolving portfolio of leading-edge services
	Niche business under the radar	*Mainstream, differentiated business with energy and tension to change faster*	*Visible and respected business that defines its own future and pulls it into the present*
	Vision, Mission, Values, Customer Promise, and Employee Bond		

this context issue in mind, since if yours is a highly bureaucratic organization, you're going to find it will sabotage your pipeline unless you address this issue. Bureaucracies subvert the pipeline's effectiveness because they take accountability and authority away from managers and leaders and give it to clerks, support staffs, auditors, accountants, and the like. Leaders lose their sense of ownership, and compliance and apathy replace motivation and commitment. It doesn't matter where the bureaucrats sit, that is, at the enterprise level or group level or business level; the leader feels that "someone else makes my decisions." As a consequence, most large US corporations have a number of leaders who are just "placeholders." They aren't trying to do anything important. They go to the important meetings, like budget and strategy, so they can protect their empire, use the tickets for ball games and dinners, and have nice offices, but they don't try to improve or change anything. This loss of ownership hampers performance at all levels.

Leadership performance needs to be energized and guided by its support system, not choked and disempowered. For this reason, analyze how decision-making authority is distributed before starting to build your performance pipeline. Determine the impact bureaucracy has on managers and leaders, and if the impact is significant, realign the system so that a true sense of ownership exists and people are motivated and committed. As the following story demonstrates, such a realignment can pay significant performance dividends.

Example

An old-line insurance company decided to get into health care and investment banking as natural extensions of its main mission, risk management for its customers. Over the years, a massive corporate bureaucracy designed to provide the company with greater control had emerged in response to regulations and frequent government audits. These numerous controls didn't fit well with the health care and investment banking acquisitions. Their leaders resented the intrusion: control procedures didn't fit the transactions, and new kinds of risk had to be understood and managed. As a result, leaders of these acquired companies ignored corporate directives.

The CEO decided to redefine how the company should work. The first major decision was to write and live by enabling policies—policies that tell you what you must do to be successful rather than what you can't do. For example, the reward systems required and commonly used in insurance, health care, and investment banking are quite different from one another. A single method of rewarding performance wasn't likely to be found. Trying to have one pay program designed by the Corporate Human Resources department wasn't effective. So, the enabling policy said, in effect, "have a reward system that fits your industry [insurance, health care, investment banking] as long as it uses our principles."

The second major decision was to revamp power-and-control processes so that leaders had greater decision-making freedom as well as greater accountability. For instance, a prior review system was put into place—a system that mandated showing a plan or program to a corporate executive for discussion before implementation—but it did not give these corporate executives unilateral veto power. They could voice their objections to the CEO and his direct reports about a plan or program, but they couldn't kill it.

As a result of these and other antibureaucratic moves, this company helped its people become more effective managers. Leaders of the acquired companies embraced the enabling policies and power-and-control processes, which helped them to work faster and with greater commitment within the corporate structure.

From Electronic Self-Indulgence to Organized Communication

Your performance pipeline will clog up if people routinely abuse their electronic communication privileges. I am not a Luddite and recognize how e-mail, smart phones, and other technologies help leaders operate with greater efficiency; but too often, performance is hurt rather than helped by overindulgent electronic communicators.

In this context, it's not possible to run an uninterrupted meeting. If cell phones don't ring because participants have been ordered to mute them, then text messages silently do their damage. Addiction to e-mails, voice mails, texts, tweets, and so on is at crisis levels. One obvious performance cost is leaders' loss of face time with direct reports. Days at work start with time in the office reading and responding to one electronic message after another, and time for walking around and communicating face-to-face is diminished. Meetings are less effective because no one pays attention to the discussion for more than a few minutes at a time.

So how do we revamp our policies toward electronic communication so that it facilitates rather than detracts from performance? While I was working with a major South African company, a young man suggested some rules for e-mail. In response to my question, "What should we do about this problem?" he spent an evening drafting these possible rules:

- No copies. If you aren't a major party at interest, you shouldn't be encumbered. No one needs to know everything.

- No escalation. Your boss shouldn't get the complaint or negative judgment before you have a chance to respond.

- No more than two exchanges. If you can't resolve your situation in two e-mails each, then you must meet face-to-face.

- No e-mails between 10:00 A.M. and 2:00 P.M. Establish an e-mail-free zone during the day to give everyone some space.

- Put short answers in the header. A yes or no answer can be easily fit into the subject line so the e-mail doesn't have to be opened.

That South African company disabled its "copy all" button. Magazine articles talk about "e-mail-free Fridays." I'm not presumptuous enough to suggest that I have a solution to this ubiquitous problem, but I do know now that every organization that wants to use the performance pipeline should at least create some rules that will prevent e-mailing, cell phoning, and the like from impacting results negatively. Instilling better processes or designing jobs in ways that improve communication discipline is at least part of the answer.

From Random Growth to Disciplined Organization Building

Your organization structure may be causing your leaders to fail. Several common practices have led to poor development of leadership skills or to undervaluing leadership work. The biggest mistake is leaders, particularly at the lower levels, who have only two, three, or four direct reports. They don't have enough leadership work to fill a day let alone a week or month. Often, these positions are created as rewards for excellent technical or professional contributors. These high-performing people can't fill their week with leadership or management tasks, so they seek out technical work in order to contribute.

Example

At a leading health and beauty products company, rapid business growth was driving almost 30 percent head-count growth. The company's terrific mission and product success made it an attractive place to work. Senior management wanted to slow down hiring, though, by becoming more efficient. From work interviews with Managers of Others and Managers of Managers, it became clear that over 75 percent of the first-line management work was being done by the Managers of Managers. Managers of Others averaged 2.5 direct reports and spent 95 percent of their time doing technical work. All technical persons promoted to Manager of Others sought a replacement person for themselves even though they continued to do a significant amount of technical work. Managers of Managers were directly managing anywhere from twenty-five to fifty people even though they had not really learned how to manage. Confusion reigned and the company lost control of the effort at lower levels.

Senior management complained that they could never get what they wanted. When they asked for a modest piece of work (think Volkswagen), they always got the gold-plated version (think Mercedes). Programs that no longer fit the strategy wouldn't die because people kept working on them according to their own interpretation of the mission. This company was financially very successful because of the markup on its products, but employees were confused and were becoming unhappy, while consumers paid too much for the products. Fewer, better managers and leaders, with bigger spans of control and more emphasis on skill-building, would have been the solution. This company was acquired by another that saw and fixed the problem.

Recommendations for Improving Your Context

Many ways exist to create a better context for your performance pipeline. I've mentioned a number of them, from changing cultural elements to revamping the operating model to placing some limits on electronic communication. But I'd like to end this chapter by returning to our farming analogy. Here are some more specific recommendations:

Examine the soil regularly. Don't rely on consultants and other outsiders to tell you what is going on. Meet regularly with your people, individually or in small groups—and make sure these groups represent all levels. You should involve over 10 percent of your leaders every quarter. Ask questions like these about their jobs:

- What work is getting done in the right way, at the right time?

- What work isn't getting done or is getting done at a price that is too high?

- What helps get the work done?

- What hinders getting the work done?

- What should be changed to get the work done better, cheaper, and faster?

Don't react or make promises until you have talked to many people and can see the patterns or themes. Avoid blame or judgment because this isn't about individuals; it is about context—the soil, not the seeds. Let everyone know what you have found out, and get their reaction before doing anything. They may not have articulated exactly what they meant the first time. Invariably, you'll find issues emerging in the context categories discussed in this chapter.

Remove rocks, weeds, and other impediments to growth. Before adding anything to the context, remove things that are in the way and see what happens. It is a rare situation that requires all problems to be addressed separately. Removing some blockages can make other things go away also. Absent any other criteria, consider starting with the most frequently mentioned problem, that is, the one that is most noticed. Here are some examples of impediments and their removal:

- Leaders and managers who don't lead or manage should be assigned to positions where they can excel, or be removed if they have attitude problems.

- Groups that hoard information must be made to share promptly and completely as measured by favorable reactions from the recipients.

- Decision-making authority held at a high level should be pushed down at least on an experimental basis.

- Teams or other units that squash ideas should be required to bring forward new ideas every month.

- People who don't learn should be required to present the practices and methods used in parallel industries or customer companies.

Check that all your rows are aligned. Make sure your strategy, your organization's capability, and the competence of your people are aligned. Think of it in this way:

- What work does our strategy require us to do?

- Is that work assigned? What isn't assigned or should be reassigned?

- Do our processes, practices, and values enable us to do that work?

- Are our people doing what is needed according to strategy requirements?

Your succession planning progress is a good tool for examining alignment.

If you change the way you farm, be transparent about and committed to your new methods. Be the role model, make some noise, be specific, talk about it, follow up, measure, discuss it at staff meetings, and so on. There is a lot of clutter to get through, a lot of deep-seated practices to undo or replace, and both public and private resistance to overcome. If you are only experimenting, you will never make the changes or the resistors will make sure the experiment doesn't work.

Use the best tools available. One major strength of the Performance Pipeline is its ease of use. You can define layer by layer the outcomes you want. Everyone's change requirement can be defined and communicated in minutes, not days. The performance pipeline helps change the context, and the context helps the pipeline work effectively.

10

Enabling Layer Transitions

I n company after company, throughout the world, I have observed leaders working at the wrong level. They aren't idle; they are delivering results, but not the results they should deliver. They have been promoted, moved up, received a pay raise, but aren't doing the new work. Instead, they are clinging to the work from their previous layer. The new leaders are *not making the transition*. They are not delivering the expected results; or just as disturbingly, the results are being delivered by their boss; in turn, their boss's boss must also drop down one layer to deliver results. This downward pull raises the cost of leadership (since leaders paid to work at level x are working at level x minus 1) and locks higher-level executives in the here and now when they should be much more concerned with the future. Managers at lower levels are also pushed down and do lower-level work. While the problem is pervasive, it isn't a perfect problem. By that I mean that in any given company, some individual leaders may be working at the right layer for a number of reasons; some are working at the right layer part of the time; and some are always working at a lower layer. This variance can mask the performance problem, so don't assume that just because John and Mary are doing the right leadership work for their level that Bill and Joan are following suit. In fact, a better assumption is that at least a certain percentage of your leaders aren't doing the right work.

Creating Risk for the Person and the Business

Almost every leader makes a transition when she starts her new job. She may transition up from a lower layer or in from another company (lateral moves within a company may not require much of a transition, but they are not as common). There is no guarantee that the required skills will be developed sufficiently to enable success in the new position. Therefore, almost every leader is at professional risk until he masters the new skills and achieves the results required by his layer. If leaders are at risk, then the organization is at risk for the same reason: expected results might not be delivered at any layer.

So this isn't just a "human resources problem"; it's not an issue that can be addressed just through coaching. Transitions need to be looked at and handled like the *substantial business problem* they are. While the failure of one leader may not sink the business or the enterprise, the cumulative effect of many poor transitions or failures in very senior positions certainly will. Consider that your company may have people in leadership positions who are overpaid for the work they're doing and aren't developing the skills required for their jobs. Perhaps the biggest risk to the business comes from high-level work—defining the future and preparing for it—not being done. Businesses don't address this problem with the seriousness it deserves. Fortunately, this chapter provides you with an opportunity and the tools to address it effectively.

Figure Out What's Wrong

The Performance Pipeline can be used as a diagnostic tool to help find the problem. Fixing it requires a clear understanding of why the problem exists. We will examine some of the key reasons that people end up working at inappropriate levels. As you'll discover, sometimes the source of the problem is in the company or business; sometimes the boss is the culprit; and sometimes the new manager is responsible for the disconnect. I'll suggest a variety of solutions, but first let's focus on the problems.

Problems in the Situation

Enterprises have ways of doing things that are embedded in their culture or are accepted practices. Some of them seriously impede layer transitions.

Transition Problem #1: Choosing the wrong person

Some companies aren't good at choosing people for jobs. They don't have the performance data or the assessment methods or the courage to make the right match between an individual and a management position. They may make the safe choice rather than the right one, or they may select someone for political expediency (a customer requests the company to hire his wife's cousin). Selections based on seniority or loyalty rather than capability or potential are also common. Choosing the wrong person for the job will turn happiness into misery. People may be delighted to be selected for a key position, but when they discover that they are ill-suited for the requirements of this managerial level, they become tremendously unhappy. Mihaly Csikszentmihalyi's compelling body of work on happiness makes it clear that this state is achieved when a match exists between our challenges and our skills. Pursuing our challenges or goals with some belief in our ability to achieve them generates true happiness. Those who successfully meet their challenges, that is, produce results at their layer, are the most likely to be promoted. Becoming a leader or getting promoted to a higher layer puts happiness at risk. Until new skills are mastered and new results delivered, it is difficult if not impossible to feel there is a match. Happiness experienced in the previous position may not be felt in the new one for quite some time. If the skills never match the challenge, people will be miserable for as long as they hold their jobs, and needed results may never be delivered.

Transition Problem #2: Cultural impediments

Knowing cultures (see Chapter Nine), because they don't tolerate mistakes or not knowing the answers, make it difficult for new managers to admit that they lack knowledge or skills and to request assistance. As a result, many managers in these cultures struggle with transitions, because learning required for gaining traction in the new role has to be carried out below the executive radar. Generally knowledge is not willingly shared since it is a source of power, so the newly appointed or promoted leader might have trouble finding answers. At best the transition process will be slow and incomplete. In some instances, managers in knowing cultures end up doing their previous jobs since they lack access to skills and knowledge required to operate effectively at their new level.

In many instances, *family cultures* use seniority or loyalty as the basis for promotions rather than capability or potential. Those who have been there the longest or have supported the boss most vigorously get the promotion. Management often fails to assess ability to perform sufficiently, so promoted leaders may not be up to the new challenge. They will cling to the old work for security and safety. The company may not notice this problem if the promotions are always done on the seniority and loyalty basis. What seems "normal" may in fact be destructive to performance across the whole company.

Highly siloed cultures present a special challenge for enabling effective transitions. Silos are essentially walls that inhibit the free flow of information and block relationship formation. A lack of dialogue with other functions or organizations makes it difficult to adjust to a new layer. Transitioning managers often struggle to learn from a broader peer group, both from those outside their function and sometimes from those within it. Typically, these managers learn narrowly and dysfunctionally; they learn not to share, and they are soon part of the problem. Over time it becomes "normal" to segregate themselves from other functions or organizations in the enterprise. Job definition and expected results are truncated, not robust or complete, because their frame of reference is limited to what they can see or touch.

I should also note one other type of organizational environment that impedes performance—a *low-performing culture*. Of course, no company consciously strives for such a culture or admits that it exists, but it is more common than you might think. Its telling traits are: doing just enough, almost meeting budgets, passing reports upward that contain factual errors, and tolerating poor performers. The new leader knows, or soon learns, that "good enough is good enough." Making a full transition and delivering all the needed results isn't likely to happen since standards are low.

Transition Problem #3: Poor organization design

Many businesses and companies aren't organized very well, so roles aren't well defined; connections that enable a smooth flow of work and information aren't in place; and expected results aren't clear. One natural consequence of these conditions is poor delegation. Leaders become detail-focused out of self-defense. In order to be sure that important work will get done, they micromanage every step in the process because they don't have confidence in the organization. When companies reflexively form committees and task forces to address problems and opportunities, it's a sure sign of poor organization. When the organization works right, new challenges go to the appropriate manager and are not given to a committee or task force. Certainly these groups are warranted at times, but well-organized companies don't form them at the drop of a hat.

Newly promoted leaders in poorly organized companies find it almost impossible to transition to and work effectively at their new layer. They don't really understand the job they had, and the new job is equally ambiguous. Even more damaging to performance, the most highly skilled and productive people are usually the ones assigned to the committees and task forces. So they have one or more time-consuming special assignment, and these assignments in turn may spawn additional roles and projects. Substantial confusion and uncertainty inhibit the transition. A new title isn't enough to clarify requirements for a new role at a new layer.

Problems That Come from the Boss

The boss's role is critical to transition success and helping people perform at peak capacity, yet as we'll see, they don't perform their role effectively for two reasons.

Transition Problem #4: Negligent bosses

When I use the word *negligent*, I'm not suggesting that these bosses neglect to talk to their recently promoted people about expectations, goals, challenges, the strategy, problems, and people to meet. Bosses are often negligent, however, when it comes to addressing the transition requirements: what to leave behind, what will be different, required changes in how time should be spent, and the consequences of not making the transition. Newly appointed leaders also find it difficult to bring up these topics—they don't want to be seen as uncertain or weak during that first conversation with their boss—and so these important issues don't surface completely. It is incumbent on bosses to initiate these conversations, and given that they once went through the same transition themselves, they should know the importance of talking about these subjects.

Just as significant, the boss orchestrated the selection process for the position and therefore should have a good sense of the promoted person's strengths and deficiencies for the new position. There won't be a better time to discuss these assets and liabilities than day one. When bosses don't take advantage of this knowledge in a timely manner, it's negligence, since new managers need to know in what ways they aren't prepared to perform at the level. Then they can do something about it.

Transition Problem #5: Overwhelming with information

Bosses sometimes overwhelm a new or newly appointed leader with too much information. In most cases, bosses commit this sin in two distinct circumstances: when the new leader is supposed to be a savior and is hired to fix many problems; and when the boss is overloaded or feels overwhelmed due to tough market conditions, declining business performance, or an underperforming team. Full disclosure during the selection process in troubled situations is rare, so many new leaders find themselves hit with a ton of bad news on day one of the new job. Typically, these leaders respond to the dire situation by doing the urgent rather than the important. They rush to clean things up rather than take the time to think through the transition and set the appropriate agenda. New leaders often jump on treadmills that they can't get off, and they are too hurried and harried to perform at their level.

Problems That Come from the Person Just Promoted

Digging in to a new job can be exciting, fun, and motivational, or it can be threatening, frightening, and overwhelming. Many newly appointed leaders or first-time leaders react in highly emotional ways, even when their bosses deal with things in a pragmatic, unemotional manner. Very difficult challenges emerge because intense feelings can cloud judgment and cause people to act irrationally.

Transition Problem #6: Doesn't want the job

People who are successful, enjoy their work, and connect well with coworkers look "promotable." So they get asked to move up. Most people accept offers to be managers at higher levels because of the status, money, and power associated with these new positions, but consciously or not, they may not want to do the new work. They may have loved the work and their colleagues at their previous position, and feel like they've been "coerced" into accepting a promotion. Lacking the motivation to learn, grow, and tackle unfamiliar or difficult assignments, they perform adequately at best. What they don't do is perform at the level required.

Transition Problem #7: Doesn't value the new work

People who are educated or trained in a particular discipline, successful in that discipline, and rewarded or recognized for that success are unlikely to give it up. Moving into management for the first time or moving up into higher-level management roles doesn't mean that they willingly let go of what's been meaningful to them for years. First-time managers especially struggle with this issue though it often occurs at higher layers as well. Working with customers, touching the product or services personally, analyzing the numbers, and bringing in new talent are usually highly valued. Consequently, most people judge their worth on their work in these areas. Teaching, coaching, giving feedback, working on the future with no short-term output, and dealing with poor performers aren't usually valued as highly in most organizations. To perform at the appropriate level, therefore, often requires a fundamental change in work values; at higher managerial levels, teaching, coaching, and so on are crucial. If the work values don't change, the work performed will not change.

Transition Problem #8: Can't relate to peers

Despite the improvements in status, the new peer group may not be much fun to be with compared to the prior one, or they may be less effective as a team. Whatever the reason, a distance exists between newly named leaders and their groups. Frequently, people just starting in an unfamiliar leadership position no longer see themselves as a member of the club; they are missing the camaraderie that existed in their previous job. In fact, this belief that they are on the outside looking in may stem from a previous experience with a boss at this layer—the new leader was poorly managed by this boss or had negative experiences with someone else at this layer. Consequently, the newly promoted manager will revert to the previous work and associate with old friends. The transition is lost at that point.

Transition Problem #9: Narcissism

Some leaders take on their new jobs and call for a stop to all work until they understand what is going on and approve it or agree with it. Subordinates usually find this frustrating or destructive; they find that the tasks they believe are important have been scuttled by a "neophyte." Leaders who halt work in this way want to get comfortable, knowledgeable, and in control, yet they fail to realize that they're making the job "all about them" rather than the other people in the group. When they conduct painful reviews, demand rejustification of projects, and go over a lot of old ground, they alienate their people. Even worse, narcissistic leaders usually don't notice the pain they are causing. Thus, the enmity they create hurts their acceptance as the leader and often lowers the performance of their people.

Transition Problem #10: Focusing on the big idea too soon

It is very tempting to start a big new job by making pronouncements about great new strategies and plans. "Things are going to be different around here" seems to be a favorite opening line, particularly in higher-level positions. Pronouncements like these elicit fear, anger, euphoria, enthusiasm, or uncertainty. There isn't any guarantee that the desired effect will be achieved. Focusing energy on the big ideas rather than addressing performance obstacles or fixing problems may hurt results. Execution often requires getting the small things right, and when everyone is focused on learning the new big picture, little things slip through the cracks. In addition, direct reports may not throw themselves into work on the big idea until they understand what it involves and accept their part in it. I'm not suggesting here that leaders should eschew big idea thinking, just that they need a reasonable break-in period before springing it on their new direct reports.

Transitions and Neuroscience

For almost forty years I have been looking for ways to help people make transitions successfully. Behavioral science was of some help but never answered the core question, "Why don't newly appointed leaders do the right job?" Logically, it shouldn't be that difficult; specific requirements can be identified with a little effort. Yet all types of people—the motivated and less motivated, the smartest and the slowest—often struggle to deliver the performance required of them. The Leadership Pipeline certainly helped diagnose problems, but something was going on in people's brains and driving counterproductive behaviors that I didn't understand.

At a CEO's off-site meeting outside Sydney, Australia, I shared facilitation of the program with Peter Burow. Peter is an author and consultant, based in Brisbane, who has focused on the application of neuroscience at work and in personal life. Most neuroscientists focus on understanding how the brain works, not on applying the learning. Peter is one of the few working on practical application of the insights in the corporate world. I really appreciated his information. Working together, we have come up with a dynamic tool that facilitates transitions to new layers. This tool takes into consideration how the brain works, recognizing why some behavior (such as failing to deliver results at a given level) doesn't appear to be rational.

The brain has both a rational system and an intuitive or emotional system. The rational brain is used to deal with new situations that we have never experienced before. In contrast, the emotional or intuitive brain enables us to respond quickly to routine situations by allowing us to access emotional memories of similar situations in the past and apply what we did last time almost instantly to the current situation. While the rational brain is slow and deals with one thing at a time, applying learned principles or frameworks, the emotional brain is fast but often gets it wrong because it assumes the new situation is a carbon copy of an old one. Both systems influence the choices we make.

In practical terms, the events in the world around us are usually filtered by the emotional system first. If the situation is brand new, as in new work at a new layer, the information is sent to the rational system for evaluation and the development of an appropriate situational response. If this new response lines up with past experience, the individual will translate the new idea into action. If, however, no similar action has been experienced and the anticipated outcome is unfamiliar, the new idea will often stay frozen in the rational part of the brain as an intention or an idea. Only when the emotional part of the brain feels comfortable will behavior change to align with the new idea. To act without emotional validation is often referred to as being outside the comfort zone, and it takes courage.

If an employee is promoted and the new environment looks and feels like the one he has just come from, the new challenges may simply bypass the rational brain and instead access the habitual centers of the emotional brain—and there is no change in behavior. This explains why people who are not transitioning properly don't seem to be behaving rationally, that is, not doing their job. What they are doing appears to be consistent with the logic and habitual patterns around the old job—and is usually completely unconscious.

The remedy for this lies in using a sequenced approach that helps individuals integrate their rational and emotional systems in a way that fosters the desired change in behavior. This means taking people out of their habitual comfort zone and creating an environment that gives them the ability to make the shift. The brain has six primary functional networks or "needs" in this change process. If all six are addressed in the right sequence, the change takes place. However, most of us focus on just one or two needs that we are aware of, leaving the other four or five unsatisfied, and so we get "stuck" along the way. This gives rise to an emotional core belief pattern that gives us certainty about life at the expense of our flexibility. We dig in rather than change, and feel very strongly about why this is the right thing to do. For a more complete treatment of this subject read *NeuroPower* by Peter Burow.

The MEALER Model

The model Peter and I have developed for helping people transition from one layer to the next comprises six phases. The central idea is to address the individual's needs in the order that they emerge so that the emotional and rational parts of the brain work in unison and the individual feels comfortable about the transition we are asking him to make. By addressing these emotional and rational needs in a structured way, we can engage the person on a transformative journey from an individual contributor to a Manager of Others, or a Function Manager to a Business Manager, and so on. We have to break down the emotional resistance to this transformation.

Our process has six steps (see Figure 10.1):

1. *Meaning*   The individual builds meaning for the company and for himself through absolute role clarity and a new identity. The performance pipeline provides the role clarity. The required identity—being not one of the gang but a leader of the gang and one of the leaders—has to be transitioned right at the beginning. To feel that we belong is our most basic need, and we develop our identity largely on the basis of where we feel most accepted and valued. This means that bonding with his new layer is critical to the individual's transition. Do this badly, and the individual will believe he is unique and "special" ("I'm not like them") so

Value Creation			Value Realization		
Meaning	Engagement	Action	Learning	Embedding	Reinvigoration
The individual gets meaning for the company and himself through absolute role clarity and a new identity.	The individual uses the knowledge and power of the position to empower others, and resists the temptation to compete with them. This involves being less egocentric and more centered on the needs and aspirations of the team. The performance problems and obstacles are defined and solved in ways that facilitate teamwork and team performance.	The individual creates a clear course of action, makes her intentions known, and creates opportunities for the team. She has the courage to take action that translates the strategy or operating plans into appropriate results-oriented actions.	The individual reflects, thinks, and adjusts on the basis of feedback. He conquers his fear of failure. This involves clearly identifying the relevant business or personal principles and role requirements, and using them rather than politics to drive plans.	The individual finds ways to embed in the business team training and systems gains that have been made at previous phases. She looks at the successes and duplicates them throughout.	The individual runs the risk of complacency (when he doesn't want to lose what he has, but anything else seems like a lot of hard work). Instead, he moves from potential disillusionment to being discerning of future goals as well as personal strengths and weaknesses. He discovers the energy for reinvigoration.

Selfishness

Fear

Indifference

Overcome three critical "sins" of personal transition

Figure 10.1 The Six Phases of the Personal Transition
Source: NeuroPower and Drotter Human Resources.

the transition he is required to make to the next layer just doesn't apply to him.

2. *Engagement*   The individual uses the knowledge and the power of the position to empower others and resists the temptation to compete with them. This involves being less egocentric and more centered on the needs and aspirations of the team. The performance problems and obstacles are defined and solved in ways that facilitate teamwork and team performance. Overcoming selfish or narcissistic tendencies is critical at this stage. The strength and value of teamwork has to be understood and internalized. The individual's realization of her own narcissism and willingness to let this go rarely happens without outside support. Some help and assistance from the boss or HR may be needed and is certainly recommended. Do this badly, and the individual will start competing with her team.

3. *Action*   The individual then creates a clear course of action and makes his intensions known. Courage is required to take actions that translate the strategy or operating plans into appropriate results-oriented actions. Action as the third step is one of the ideas that make this model different. Action that is not anchored in doing the right work at the right layer or not focused on empowering the team leads to early disaster. If this step is not done well, the new leader becomes bullying and demanding and becomes the impossible boss— burning out staff, taking unduly high risks, and driving the team into the ground.

4. *Learning*   The individual reflects, thinks, and adjusts according to feedback. She must conquer the fear of failure. This involves clearly identifying the relevant business or personal principles and role requirements and using them rather than politics to drive plans. The actions taken in step 3 provide real-life experience, which the individual and the

team, boss, and peers can use for learning. By being open to feedback, the learning about what works and what doesn't, provides powerful motivation for going forward in the right way and working on the right things. If this step is done badly, the new leader becomes paranoid and stops sharing information within the team, and instead focuses on politics and managing up. Performance drops as politics and siloing information become the focus of attention.

5. *Embedding*   The individual finds ways to embed in the business or organization, team-appropriate training and method improvements on gains that have been made. The individual looks at successes and duplicates them throughout. This is where real improvements in productivity or capability become institutionalized. If this step is done badly, the wrong models and approaches are duplicated. Rather than duplicating success, teams may play to the ego of the leader, or the leader merely duplicates things he enjoys.

6. *Reinvigoration*   The individual runs the risk of complacency when he doesn't want to lose what he has and new goals seem too hard. He may have achieved the original goals established for him by the boss or by the strategy. He has to move to new and probably tougher goals so that performance will continue to get better. He must discover the energy for reinvigoration or risk becoming just another plateaued "placeholder."

As you can see, the transformation process required for making a layer transition is complicated and challenging. Some can do it on their own, but most need the guidance of a supportive boss and the help of a trained HR person. Transition doesn't end in a week or a month. It should continue until new goals are established and met as a matter of natural process. Fortunately, it has been well proven that the brain can and will evolve. The wiring isn't fixed.

There is one last complication. Each step builds on, encompasses, and transcends the previous. This suggests that the meaning step establishes the terms of the engagement, which in turn determines the action and the learning and finally the embedding. From this perspective, meaning is the most critical of the steps and sadly the one botched most often.

The common error is to focus on the action and learning steps rather than getting the meaning and engagement steps right. This flawed method for transition creates the short-term illusion of success through activity but quickly descends into firefighting—and no transition. Beware of transition plans that are all "action."

Recommendations for the Boss

Bosses who have hired transitioning leaders have primary responsibility for making these transitions work, yet many of them do little more than dump information on new leaders and check in on progress irregularly. Whether they believe it's up to individuals to make it on their own or they are uncertain what to do to ease the transition, they often fail in their responsibility. To enable the transition using the Performance Pipeline and MEALER Model, here are eight steps that will prove useful:

1. Treat the transition like the business problem it is. You may be creating management risk through your current actions—or inaction. Think it through, put time on your calendar, have a plan, let the new person know what to expect from you, and be supportive. Consider all you would do for a new and very important customer. The new employee can make your life pleasant or miserable.

2. Use this transition as an opportunity to make needed changes. Tell the current team individually and collectively

how you feel about their performance and what they need to change (if anything). Get rid of unnecessary work, terminate projects that aren't going anywhere, move on poor performers, and get really clear about roles and responsibilities. Build a performance pipeline to help create clarity for everyone.

3. Make sure you are working at the right level. Examine your calendar objectively to see where your time really goes. Delegate the lower-level work that you enjoy but shouldn't do. Have a talk with your boss about this and agree that you will both work at the right layer.

4. Get some help from HR, and use the MEALER Model. HR should be able to participate in many of the sessions and help you judge the new person's progress. Be sure you understand and accept the MEALER Model. HR should fill in when you can't participate.

5. Get involved from the first minute the new person is in the job. Communicate the results you expect and when you expect them. Go over the MEALER Model with him so that he will understand how the transition process will work. Introduce him to the HR people who will be providing assistance. Let him know that output from him isn't expected until he has established meaning and engaged properly.

6. Deal with the naysayers and others who might not cooperate. Make it clear that the new leader is your choice, has your support, and should be given a chance to prove herself. Talk with those who have expressed an interest in the job but weren't selected. Help them see what their future opportunity might be. In siloed cultures, reach across the wall to help improve connections with other organizations for the new person and for the rest of your team.

7. Create a community in which individuals can undertake and experience transformation. There may be others on the team who have been at their level for a while but have not transitioned properly. Everyone needs to be at the right layer to maximize the value of your team.

8. Control the urge to dump every bit of information on the new person on day one. Think through how the information should be clustered and sequenced for best understanding. Check if the person is grasping the requirements from the first discussion before starting the second one.

Recommendations for the Individual

Ideally, you'll be working in concert with your boss to make the transition. Even if your boss isn't on board with this method, though, you can do a number of things to help yourself:

1. Learn the MEALER Model, and work your way through it. Doing it with your boss would be best, but if he isn't available or willing, then find a friend, mentor, or HR professional to be your partner as you work your way through. Pay particular attention to finding meaning and redefining your identity.

2. Avoid early pursuit of the "big idea." Don't make major pronouncements about big changes or big results that you plan to deliver. Instead, focus on solving problems and removing barriers to performance that your people identify. Build goodwill with them early by showing them you care about their problems.

3. Be aware of your emotional state. Fear of failure, self-righteousness about the new role, feelings of not belonging with your new peer group, desire for revenge, and apathy or complacency are all possible in this new situation. Stay

focused on the transition process defined in the MEALER Model. Ask for feedback about what feelings show and how that is being received.

4. Don't compete with your people. You have more power, more information, and more access, so it is a rigged game. Let them do their work, and encourage them to be great. Their success is your success.

5. Require measurement and feedback on what you do and what the team does. Learn from the successes and the failures. Experiment and innovate wherever possible to find the best way of getting the required results.

6. Don't get stuck on solving problems. Do some problem solving early, but when progress starts to be made, work on replicating what works throughout your organization.

7. Don't declare victory too early. It takes time to master a new layer. Keep striving to get better. Otherwise you may become just a placeholder living on past success and treading water.

8. Learn to see the layer through the eyes of your peer group. They have experience that you lack. Actions and behaviors are understood best through their eyes, so learn what they are trying to do and don't just go with what you observe or hear on your own.

Recommendations for Human Resources

Human Resources is best able to assist with layer transition when they understand the transformation process and are clear about the required results for the person they are helping. These steps will help HR in both areas:

1. Get certified in the MEALER Model so that you can support the boss and the person properly by asking the right questions and making the right suggestions.

2. Work with the boss to get your own sense of the required results before the person shows up. (It is possible that you have already done this as part of the selection process.)

3. Get involved at the same time the boss does—that is, from the minute leaders start their jobs. Standard practice has been to give people some time to settle in. In truth, they are most receptive to your help on the first day. Their understanding of the job may be incorrect or incomplete, and it is less threatening to ask HR than to ask the boss.

4. Stay involved as a sounding board or as a coach. Engage the boss when needed. This process isn't finished until the new person is successful.

Tying It All Together

Transitioning to a new layer is difficult and risky for the person and for the business. Success in transitions shouldn't be left to chance. The hiring manager and HR should collaborate to make sure the transition happens in an orderly way with appropriate speed. Consider the person's situation against the ten reasons transitions may be difficult. Decide which one(s) apply. Start from that point to work with the person, their new peers, and other parts of the organization to remove obstacles, help the person understand what performance is needed, explain the MEALER Model, and work through the transition steps. Remember, the transition isn't complete until the person has achieved the first set of goals and is tackling a more challenging set. Performance should continue to get better, not plateau.

11

Implementing Your Performance Pipeline

Throughout the book, I've detailed the purpose and key results that must be achieved at each layer. Just knowing what these results are, making results expectations known to the right people at the right layers, and rewarding those who deliver or exceed these results can help you create a performance pipeline. Realistically, however, I recognize that translating concepts from paper to practice can be challenging. As much as I've tried to offer information and ideas to facilitate implementation, I know that the real world has a way of throwing you curves that aren't addressed in books.

For this reason, I'd like this final chapter to focus on what you should do to make the Performance Pipeline useful and effective. Here are the six keys to pipeline implementation:

- Get your philosophy about performance right

- Build your own tailored performance pipeline

- Commit to and execute motivational performance discussions

- Engage at all levels, not just your direct reports

- Get HR to understand and accept needed changes

- Pursue performance improvement relentlessly

Getting Your Philosophy Right

Your philosophy—what you believe about people at work, their purpose, their motivation, their likely success, and how hard they work—causes you to pursue performance in a particular way. If you aren't getting the performance you desire from your team or your business, then you have to make changes. If your philosophy stays the same, your changes won't last, no matter how well they work initially. Frameworks and principles are more effective than rules and policies. The former provide the flexibility necessary for people to make their own choices. In the twenty-first century, people respond with greater enthusiasm and creativity when treated as informed participants; they see the results they and their people should shoot for and choose to find their own ways to generate these results. Rules and policies, on the other hand, demonstrate rigidity; they force people to do what you say is good for them. Forcing people to follow the Performance Pipeline as if it were the "law of the land" only encourages lawbreaking.

The Performance Pipeline is a framework for determining what should be delivered at each layer, and it works best when it is implemented as a flexible framework rather than as doctrine. To approach it flexibly, the following principles are useful:

PRINCIPLE #1: *We are all here to get the work done.*

Business is competitive. At this very moment, people in other companies are sitting in meetings trying to figure out how to steal your customers, pirate your best people, and leapfrog your products. Everyone has to stay focused on what is important. Let competition take their eyes off the real purpose for being at work by seeking higher status, acquiring more power, and building empires. Focus your efforts on adding value by getting the work done, that is, delivering results required at your layer. The Performance Pipeline flows best when we all concentrate on the results that are required from our particular level.

PRINCIPLE #2: *Results (adding value) must be differentiated by layer.*
Too much work exists requiring too many different skills for every leader to be doing the same thing. We need to differentiate between working on the present and working on the future. We also need to differentiate between strategic work, operational work, and tactical work. Defining the performance pipeline makes clear the required differentiation and what work should be done where. It is a guide for the whole organization.

PRINCIPLE #3: *Conversation about work should be motivational not judgmental.*
After talking with bosses and colleagues, we should be enthusiastic about delivering. Most performance appraisals, however, demotivate. We feel personally judged and respond with thoughts like, "He doesn't know what I am up against" and "He doesn't know what I've done" and "He is the problem." To be motivated, we need to talk frequently about performance, that is, what has been done, what is next, and how best to do it so everyone has the same view. What isn't motivational is lamenting a slow rate of progress, getting personal ("You're not trying"), and discussing performance comprehensively only once or twice a year. Therefore, approach the performance pipeline as a tool to motivate rather than as a method of passing judgment.

PRINCIPLE #4: *Reward and recognition decisions require objectivity and situational analysis.*
The performance pipeline is a contextual tool. In other words, it's designed to adapt to a given environment (rather than demand that the environment adapt to it). Therefore, the more you see it from a situational and objective standpoint, the more effective it will be. Let's say you achieve 90 percent of the goal. What were the circumstances? Acts of nature, market shifts, collapse of the financial

sector, competitors' innovations, and other extenuating circumstances may well suggest that 90 percent was a heroic result. Conversely, exceeding budget by 5 percent when the market is up by 10 percent is not great performance. Therefore, embrace objective, situational analysis before deciding what pay increases should be or whether to promote someone or draw conclusions about an individual's achievements (or lack thereof). Don't be swayed by relationship baggage, obsolete information, or political pressure. Ask questions to understand the context as well as the outcome. Slavish adherence to budgets (best guess made eighteen months ago) doesn't help, particularly in rapidly changing environments. If you're using the pipeline to assess how well someone performed, be aware that you must take the results at a given level with a grain of salt. Given the situation, one person may have performed at an exceptional level by delivering three out of five results, while another person who delivered four of five may have performed only competently, considering all the resources at his disposal. Over the course of two or three years all the results should be achieved.

Building Your Own Tailored Pipeline

Don't try to force your business or enterprise into the Performance Pipeline. Rather, tailor the pipeline to fit your company. You may not have all the layers that we discussed, so you have to redistribute the work. If you don't have Group Managers, redistribute those results to the CEO and the Business Managers. If your enterprise is only one business, you won't have Group Managers and the CEO functions as both the Business Manager and CEO. Feel free to reorganize the layers if it seems beneficial.

Tailoring means using the language and the terminology of your business or enterprise. Substitute your own position titles, for example, Region Executive instead of Group Manager, Unit Manager instead of Manager of Managers, as I've used in my model. For authenticity and relevance, rely on your key business terms in the performance standards part of the pipeline. These standards need to be instantly credible and recognizable. If you want to tell your organization that you need to see some change, using new language helps.

Just about every set of performance standards has a standard that says "met all goals and budgets." The performance pipeline is designed to dovetail with your planning and goal-setting process, not replace it. Attach the goals, KPIs, budgets, and so on to the standards to create a complete definition of expected results. This combination makes an effective position description and can be updated quickly as plans change.

Conducting Motivational Performance Discussions

The performance pipeline gains increased value through conversation. It's not an esoteric human resources tool but one that really comes to life when direct reports and bosses discuss expected contributions and when they review performance. These discussions should take place at the beginning of a new measurement period or at the start of a new job, clarifying exactly what is expected. After these initial conversations, additional conversations should take place and lead to a measurement discussion.

If you think back to the four principles above, you'll understand why these discussions should be motivational. In order to get work done, to get the right results at the right layer, and so on, we need to be challenged and encouraged. This is opposed to the typical performance review discussion with a boss, which is often demotivating and discouraging. Bosses who are poorly prepared for these conversations, who rely on opinions rather than facts, who fail to recognize the change in context, or who are too personal in their criticisms generally don't motivate. There is a better way, and it is actually easy to do. I suggest you take advantage of the opportunity for great discussions that the Performance Pipeline model presents by following a few simple steps:

- *Have a thorough discussion every month.* If you want the whole job done, you have to discuss the whole job frequently. The status of a project, the closing of a sale, the completion of a plan, and many other events entail numerous, evolving conversations—things change, and conversations need to be held to go over these changes. Monthly discussions with the whole team to review progress against budgets and goals are necessary. I am suggesting that you take one more step and review individuals in the same monthly manner.

Discussing performance at the end of the first month is particularly valuable because there are eleven months left to fix any problems. At the end of the second month there are still ten months left to fix any problems. Your purpose is getting the work done. Year-end discussions don't serve this purpose.

Have a thorough discussion of all the items in the performance standards along with goals and KPIs. Convey the importance of doing the whole job, not just those hot-button items you talk about anyway. These holistic discussions teach many young (and even older) managers the value of developing people or working on a future project while pursuing production goals. No matter what you say about doing the whole job, your people will take their cue from what you ask about.

- *Collect evidence, not opinions, every month.* At the monthly discussion, put into writing the key things that got done. Table 11.1 is an example of what this report might look like by year-end. The performance standards provide a framework for this approach. Put

Table 11.1 Pipeline Performance Evaluation, Manager of Others

Shift in Work Values
- From results personally to getting results through others
- From valuing own success to valuing the success of others

Name: Johanna Johnson
Title: Mgr. 1 Audits
Date: 12/15/09
Period Covered: 2009
Prepared by: B. Ramirez

Standards	Not Yet Full	Full	Exceptional	Rating
Operational/Technical Results				Full
• Self/team always meet targets, due dates, and quality standards	Overspent staff development budget by 10%, mostly on courses that weren't job related.	Work group met all KPIs this year. See Dec. KPI report. Work group met all goals this year due to excellent management discipline. Performance discussions held every month.	Team developed quicker methods of completing audits that are compliant with regulation, resulting in greater efficiency.	
• Reliable results produced by holding employees to agreed-upon methods and measures				
• Innovation through being technically current with state-of-the-art industry regulations and product development methods				
• Operational/technical/ professional advice to team assured achievement of goals and results				
Management	Completion of Monitoring project jeopardized by poor scheduling required extra staff resources to accomplish work on time.	Roles and accountabilities clearly defined. Open and candid dialogue conducted at least monthly. Team performance measures are linked to goals and milestones. Achievement can be clearly followed. Critique and process improvement of team's work done at weekly team meetings resulted in finding ways to cut costs by 10%. All team members are full performers.		Full
All associates have clear, current and measurable goals and objectives				
Annual plan ensured effective allocation of resources in order to reach targets/goals				
Control systems ensured timely results and no surprises				
Regular and ongoing feedback provided to direct reports				
Right people in right job at right time				
Clear picture of current performance conveyed to project team members*				
Project team members received coaching and feedback**				

(Continued)

Table 11.1 (Continued)

Standards	Not Yet Full	Full	Exceptional	Rating
Leadership • Led by example; lives to corporate values • Viable successor developed and retained • Business case for change well communicated and effectively executed • Development plans are in place for everyone and actively pursued	Cut corners on data validation in order to meet deadlines No viable backup in place Team capability not improved. Chose wrong development actions/programs	Team members had right information at the right time due to weekly planning meetings.		Not Yet Full
Relationships • Open communication with associates, peers and manager(s) • Displays fairness, exhibits trust and gains respect through own behavior and actions • Full understanding of customer needs and peer requirements sought and addressed • Proactively establish and maintain internal and external stakeholders and relationships • Listening skills to others needs, agendas and priorities		Reached out to customers at least once per month and peers on a weekly basis. Widely viewed as reliable supplier and partner.	Role model for participation in staff mtgs and design mtgs Networking with peers in industry resulted in team learning and incorporating more effective audits methods	Exceeds
Innovation • Process improvement increased productivity vs. last year • One useful innovation each year		Consistent process improvement effort by self and team. Source of ideas and improvement for peers.		Full

*For employees on project teams.

the full performance standards in the first column and capture the evidence in the following columns. Now you have a factual record. At the end of the year, the "performance rating" will be self-evident and no new effort will be required except for an overall assessment.

Gathering and Communicating Evidence

Evidence is a concept that many people misinterpret or don't grasp fully; or they don't know how to collect evidence related to performance and convey it in a motivational way. Therefore, to implement this element of motivational discussion effectively, you need to learn a bit about how to make use of performance-based evidence.

Let's start out with a definition: Evidence is composed of the results achieved and the context in which they were achieved. For example, "revenue increased 10 percent" is evidence, but "revenue increased 10 percent in a down market" or "revenue increased 10 percent in a market that grew 15 percent" are much stronger pieces of evidence. Our job is to help our people understand whether or not they added appropriate value. So, we dig for information until we also have the context right.

Evidence may be absolute, such as "operating plan was produced on time," or it may be relative, as in "operating plan was better than last year." When gathering evidence, we should add enough context to enable any reader or listener to be convinced. For relative evidence we have to say why the operating plan is better than last year: "new market research was used to direct the planning." Otherwise, the improvement statement is just an opinion.

Reporting on Evidence

The performance standards for each layer provide an effective guide to help us understand what evidence to focus on and how to judge it. That is the main reason we developed the standards.

To simplify recording of evidence, rely on the pipeline performance evaluation format that follows (or your own variation of it). Place the evidence collected during the discussion in the appropriate column. Share this format with your direct reports, so they can bring evidence in this format to your discussion.

Pipeline Performance Evidence

Standards	Not Yet Full Performance	Full Performance	Exceptional Performance
Business Results			
Met all targets and budgets.	Spent the budget but didn't upgrade the PCs as planned.		

Don't expect to have evidence for every standard, particularly when the standards are new, and because a specific job may not require them all in any given year.

Avoid statements of activities when no real results or accomplishments were achieved; for example, "visited ten districts; analyzed various processes; worked on new concept." These are activities. The trigger question should be, "What tangible difference or improvement resulted?"

Avoid general statements where the contribution is not clear, such as, "made personal contribution in process engineering" or "visualized new concept in data analysis." None of these generalities identify results, accomplishments, or outcomes.

What Should Be Discussed

Discussing the evidence first helps you and your direct reports to find common ground on the status of the work. Covering all the relevant standards (frequently there are one or two that don't apply at the moment) is the first objective but shouldn't take all the time.

Reserve the majority of the meeting for talking about *the work to be done*. More specifically, ask questions about what exactly should get done, how it will get done, what the obstacles and risks are, and what help is needed; use these questions as catalysts for the discussion. Real coaching and learning happen here. People experience accelerated development from regular conversations such as these. When you share key insights with your people, hash out how to deal with obstacles, and so on, you motivate your direct reports to perform—you give them the information and responsiveness that help them do their jobs better. Getting deeply involved before the fact rather than making judgments after the fact produces better results and helps to avoid costly mistakes and rework.

Reaching Conclusions

At the end of the measurement period you will have to reach a conclusion about the performance of this individual. To make an assessment, use the following questions:

- What does the preponderance of evidence suggest? Where is most of the evidence?

- At what level is the person assigned and at what level is he performing?

- What is she doing really well?

- What important items from the standards need to be improved?

- What important items from the standards is he not addressing at all?

- What should she do to move results from one column to the next, higher one?

- On balance, what overall judgment can you make about this person's performance: not yet full, full, or exceptional?

This is the toughest part of the whole process. It may be challenged later by the person. Let the evidence be your guide. Feel free to go back and collect more evidence if you feel you need it. A summing up of this type is useful for both of you. Consider doing it quarterly. *Focus on measuring the work and the results, not on judging the person.*

Engaging at All Levels

You need to know what is happening at every level in your performance pipeline. The reports you receive aren't enough. Go see for yourself what is going on and why, and then form your own opinions about the progress and state of work completion. The Performance Pipeline helps you know what questions to ask and gives you a map of what should be happening—you know the results that are targeted, so it's simply a matter of determining if people are achieving these results.

In some companies, of course, one taboo is higher-level managers talking to people at lower levels about their performance; the fear is that the managers in between will be offended by this intervention. You may have to condition your direct reports and probably their direct reports to accept this normal and necessary effort on your part to understand what is going on and what isn't getting done. Make it clear that you won't give work direction or fix problems, just gather information. Whatever you learn should be shared with the people in between.

You can engage at all levels if you ask the right questions of the right people at the right time. These questions can help you obtain information about the quality of your team as leaders, the state-of-the-work effort, and the problems and obstacles that exist. Remember, though, that you should not ask these questions in a way that puts people on the spot or suggest they should pass judgment on their boss. Keep the questions simple and neutral in tone. For instance:

- Tell me about your development plan. Where do you stand on completing it?

From their answer you can learn whether they have one or not, what their development needs are, whether they are growing, and what results might be in jeopardy due to shortfalls in skills or experience.

- What have you gotten done in the last three or six or nine months that you are really proud of?

You will hear about results, or you will hear about activity. If they are proud of activities, then the results orientation isn't in place or isn't strong enough. You will also hear about their work values. All of this will help you understand if they are working at the right level.

- What are your biggest obstacles, and how do you deal with them?

You will probably hear about problems that haven't surfaced at your level—problems that would otherwise escape your notice. You will also hear about your people's ingenuity and problem-solving skills or the lack thereof.

These questions are just three of many you can ask (and ask in your own way). As you formulate queries that will help you engage at all levels, keep in mind that you are a power figure to those at lower levels. Your presence can be motivational, or you can be threatening to them. So, put them at ease, and don't ask them to judge their boss, because they won't do it. Encourage them to do their best no matter what you find.

Validate what you hear with the managers in between you and those interviewed. Listen closely to what they say before planning any remedial actions. You are trying to motivate better achievement, not demotivate anyone.

Getting HR to Understand and Accept the Pipeline

In every company I have worked with on the performance pipeline, a core group of HR practitioners have been part of the work as well as enthusiastic partners. Some people, though, have been resistant, suspicious, resentful, and frequently passive-aggressive. Although other functions and senior management have embraced the Pipeline methodology, this model threatens many long-established HR tools and practices, which have been these practitioners' focus and method for adding value.

You may thus encounter some resistance from your HR people, and if so, they need to be brought along, reassured, and educated. For example, if you use the performance standards with goals, you can eliminate position descriptions. Many will find that threatening, because they work on position descriptions. Defining pay grades isn't needed, because the pipeline layers should have one pay grade each, with a broad pay range. Existing pay grades may not seem logical when the rigor of the pipeline is applied. Systems thinking is required to work effectively with the pipeline, and many HR practitioners are trained in transactional work. Therefore, plan to train HR people in pipeline methods, and allow them to practice using it—if they're sharp, they'll recognize its value not only to the company but to the facilitation of HR's tasks. Ideally, you'll have other functions in the room when you train HR to use the pipeline. HR should hear the reception other functions and business leaders give the Performance Pipeline. That reception has been positive in every single company; there will be support for HR to lead the implementation. Hold specific discussions about changes in programs to support the Performance Pipeline. It is likely that some improvements in job definition, succession planning, leadership development programs, coaching, and so on can be achieved.

Pursuing Performance Improvement Relentlessly

The success of the performance pipeline comes about most quickly when management at all layers is committed to performance improvement. Lukewarm support won't cut it. Leaders must believe that great performance is possible anywhere, anytime, in any business. What seems to make the most difference are leaders who won't settle for less. A few basic tools like the performance pipeline coupled with genuine commitment can work wonders. I have seen businesses of all sizes transform from low performance to best in class on the strength of genuine commitment by their leaders.

No matter what level of performance you now enjoy (or worry about), this level will fluctuate. Great performance one year is often followed by overwhelming competitive response, and your performance declines. Or the stars align, resources are abundant, and you find your performance rebounding after a mediocre year. You can't control external conditions that impact performance, but you can control how you pursue performance. Relentless pursuit of performance improvement is particularly important in uncertain business conditions. Perfection isn't the objective; offering better products and services than the competition is the goal. The clarity and focus that a performance pipeline offers have to be supported by leaders at all layers who strive to get better every day personally, and who enable the success of the people below them.

Conclusion

Implementing a performance pipeline takes effort and commitment. All the companies I have worked with, without exception, have told me about the various benefits they have derived. In their view, the performance pipeline is well worth the effort.

Deciding what benefits you want and need is key. Understanding that the Performance Pipeline is a framework—a tool—to help you achieve those benefits will allow you to maintain your focus and energy. The Performance Pipeline isn't an end in itself; it is a means to an end: achieving your desired business performance.

The pervasive uncertainty businesses are living with requires all leaders to improve their effectiveness. The Performance Pipeline can provide them with the clarity and focus that are so critical to their success. Every company can benefit when all leaders effectively pull in the same direction. When leaders help those below them succeed, everyone is a winner.

Please let me know how you do, so that you and I can both learn from your effort.

Tool 1

Actual Performance Pipeline
from Company E

Group Manager

Shift in Work Values

- From results through a multifunctional business to results through regional capability
- From business competitive advantage to regional leverage
- From shareholder value to stakeholder value
- From long-term strategic plans to strategic frameworks
- From valuing all functions to valuing all businesses

Results	Full Performance	Exceptional Performance	Skills, Knowledge, and Experience
Business/Functional Results • Regional profit, economic profit • Regional sales, volume • Region product portfolio • Value proposition • Region positioning • Economic environment	• Planned short-term Regional results (volume, profit, ROI) delivered without compromising long-term growth • Competitive advantage sustainable across Region • Economic, political, competitive, market and industry knowledge evident in strategic framework • Each Country met all KBIs • Each Country made a direct contribution to Regional leverage	• Profit grows faster than revenue for the Region • Competitive advantage achieved through leveraging resources • KBI achievement exceeded all other Regions • Each country met all targeted results	• Balancing risks • Understanding of financial impact of decisions in each Country • Strategic planning; deep knowledge of the contribution of each Country • Multi-Country experience • Ability to think strategically • Experience in running a Country • Must know how to read and interpret Regional market data and competitive response
Management • Operational planning • Organizational structure • Quality • Strategic problem solving • Productivity • Resource tradeoffs • Portfolio management	• Product quality consistently at or above standard across Region • Tradeoff decisions assured all Countries met plans • Best practice transfer improved every Country • Portfolio adjustments enabled Region to improve competitive advantage	• Organizational energy superior to other Regions • Business practices emulated by competition and other Regions • Productivity improved year after year	• Ability to manage a portfolio • Experience managing through Business leaders • Ability to make hard decisions among good choices and courage to stay the course • Contingency planning experience • Willingness to rely on and have confidence in Country leaders to achieve results • Ability to shift resources to address problems • Ability to anticipate and avoid problems

Leadership
- Portfolio strategy
- Personal leadership
- Pipeline development
- Enable Business leadership
- Performance culture
- Strategic vision; strategy
- Social responsibility
- OpCo success

- Portfolio strategy delivered competitive advantage; understood and accepted by the employees and the Company
- "A" performance delivered by every Country and teamwork evident
- Role model for OpCo participation
- Ready now successors in place at every level
- Lives corporate values
- Right person in right job and poor performers addressed quickly at all levels
- Each country had an approved strategy

- Role model for living corporate values and directives
- Countries performs with or without involvement of Regional Director
- Opportunities for partnering with community/ government actively leveraged

- Developing portfolio strategy
- Coaching and mentoring Business leaders
- High integrity
- Ability to select and assess Business leaders based on business strategy
- Knowing how to build alliances in order to get things done
- Ability to create a future that people want to be a part of

Relationship Results
- Key customer relationships
- Subordinate and senior executive relationships
- Peer relationships
- Company spokesperson
- Government relationships including local and national

- Customer interface includes joint long-term planning Regional planning
- Strong working relationships with each Country Manager and OpCo member
- Climate supported relationship building at all levels and throughout the Region
- Government relationships enabled favorable treatment and early warning including prospective Countries
- Results achieved in ways that helped other Regions succeed

- Ideas and insight sought by community and government leaders for advancement of their initiatives
- Sought out by peers for coaching and strategic thinking

- Building relationships for their own sake
- Ability to understand what drives Business leaders and Country political leaders
- Ability to read powerful people and complex situations
- Confident in a leadership role
- Understands the greater good
- Knowledge of political agendas in the Region's governments

Growth and Innovation Results
- New markets
- Acquisitions
- New products
- New customers
- New methods and processes

- Business processes continually improved and exploited growth opportunities and/or lowered cost
- Each Country Manager implemented two innovations
- Acquisitions improved portfolio's long-term growth and profit potential

- Breakthrough results achieved through industry leading innovative portfolio management
- Acquisitions seamlessly integrated

- Experience in creating a climate for innovation
- Ability and willingness to exploit new markets
- Open-minded and tolerant of difference
- Willingness to experiment and try new things
- Experience with negotiating and integrating acquisitions
- Ability to take short-term risks to enable long-term gain

Business Manager

Shift in Work Values

- From results through a function to results through a multifunctional business team
- From functional state-of-the-art results to business competitive advantage
- From functional excellence to shareholder value
- From planning for functional results to creating long-term strategic plans
- From valuing your own function to valuing all functions

Results	Full Performance	Exceptional Performance	Skills, Knowledge, and Experience
Business/Functional Results • Profit, economic profit • Sales, volume • Competitive analysis • Value proposition • Resource strategy • Economic environment	• Planned short-term business results (volume, profit, ROI) delivered without compromising long-term growth • Competitive advantage sustainable • Value proposition met and anticipated customer needs and CO. E. needs • Economic, political, competitive, market and industry knowledge evident in strategy and decision making • All KBIs met • Each Function made a direct contribution to competitive advantage	• Profit grows faster than revenue • Competitive advantage achieved through innovation • KBI achievement exceeded all other countries	• Risk taking and risk management • Understanding of financial impact of decisions • Business planning; deep knowledge of the contribution of each function • Multifunctional experience • Ability to think tactically and strategically • Able to think in terms of profitability and sustainability rather than functional capability • Must know how to read and interpret market data and competitive response
Management • Operational planning • Organizational structure • Quality • Strategic problem solving • Execute strategy • Safety • Organization effectiveness • Productivity	• Business strategy executed at optimal cost • Organizational energy directed toward achieving business results • Functional activity fully integrated and aligned through the operational plan (boundaryless) • Reviews (project reviews, budget, plan reviews) drive decisions rather than share information • Product quality consistently at or above standard	• Organizational energy superior to peers and competitors • Business practices emulated by competition and peers • Productivity improved year after year	• Experience managing through several layers • Ability to make hard decisions and courage to stay the course • Contingency planning experience • Willingness to rely on and have confidence in functional leaders to achieve results • Ability to architect an organization to support strategy • Ability to anticipate and avoid problems • Ability to problem solve at the root cause level

Leadership
- Personal leadership
- Team strength
- Enable functional leadership
- Performance culture
- Strategic vision; strategy
- Company capability
- Social responsibility

- Business strategy delivered competitive advantage; understood and accepted by the employees and the Company
- "A" performance delivered by every team member and teamwork evident
- Personally connected to employees at all levels
- Ready now successor in place and talent pipeline improves each year
- Visible community leadership enhanced company's image
- Lives corporate values
- Right person in right job and poor performers addressed quickly

- Role model for living corporate values and directives
- Team performs with or without involvement of General Manager
- Opportunities for partnering with community/government actively leveraged

- Coaching and mentoring leaders
- High integrity
- Respectful of others
- Ability to select and assess functional leaders based on business strategy
- Knowing how to build alliances in order to get things done
- Ability to create a future that people want to be a part of
- Articulate communicator and effective listener at several layers

Relationships
- Key customer relationships
- Subordinate and senior executive relationships
- Peer relationships
- Company spokesperson
- Community relations
- Political relationships

- Customer interface includes joint long-term planning; cross-functional planning
- Strong working relationships with each team member and each senior executive
- Climate supported relationship building at all levels and throughout organization
- Government relationships enabled favorable treatment and early warning

- Influence and insight sought by community and industry leaders for advancement of their initiatives
- Sought out by peers for coaching and strategic thinking

- Appreciate relationships for their own sake
- Ability to understand what drives other people
- Ability to read powerful people and complex situations
- Confident in a leadership role
- Well read in current events
- Understands the greater good

Growth and Innovation
- New markets
- New applications
- Acquisitions
- New products

- Business processes continually improved and exploited growth opportunities and/or lowered cost
- Acquisitions completed based on world-class analysis and meet performance expectations
- Each senior team member implemented one innovation

- Breakthrough results achieved through industry leading strategies
- Acquisitions seamlessly integrated

- Experience in implementing innovation
- Intellectual curiosity
- Ability and willingness to exploit new markets
- Open-minded and tolerant of difference
- Willingness to take risks and to learn from mistakes
- Willingness to experiment and try new things
- Experience with negotiating and integrating acquisitions

Function Manager

Shift in Work Values

- From results through a subfunction to results through a complete function and a country team
- From subfunctional productivity to functional, state-of-the-art results
- From subfunctional integration to functional excellence
- From operational planning to planning for functional strategy, aligned with country business and corporate strategy
- From valuing your team to valuing your whole function
- From effective functional team member to effective business team member at country business and corporate levels

Results	Full Performance	Exceptional Performance	Skills, Knowledge, and Experience
Business/Financial Results • Profit, economic profit • Sales, volume • Delivery of budget • Cost/operating expense • Competitive analysis • Customer Satisfaction Index	• Planned short-term business and functional results delivered without compromising long-term strategic position (profitability/EBITA, asset utilisation/economic profit, growth/volume, ROIC, working capital, cost management, delivery, quality) • All mission critical goals/KBIs met • Function made a direct contribution to competitive advantage • Customer satisfaction improves year after year	• Function's results enabled business to exceed plan • All mission critical goals/KBIs exceeded • Targets raised during business cycle met • Function delivered industry leading competitive advantage within country business	• Functional risk taking and risk management • Understanding of financial impact of decisions • Function planning; deep knowledge of the contribution of the function • Ability to think tactically and strategically • Able to think in terms of functional sustainability rather than functional short-term wins • Must know how to read and interpret market data and competitive response • Cross-functional thinking

Management
- Strategy execution
- Execution excellence
- Organisational structure and effectiveness
- Operational planning
- Strategic problem solving
- Productivity
- Compliance (EU, SOX etc.)
- Crisis management

- Business and function strategy executed at optimal cost
- Right organisation, processes and systems in place to deliver function results
- Infrastructure effectiveness enabled business success while maintaining processes and systems
- Business performance management system and tools for cross-functional boundary management fully utilised and outcomes measured with KBIs
- Capital and other resources trade-off decisions assured all function's plans were met
- Acquisitions integrated to capture business objectives and leverage all synergies (e.g. achieving cost reduction)

- Observable organisational energy superior to peers and competitors
- Function practices copied by peers
- Planning maximized overall synergies

- Experience managing through managers
- Ability to architect a functional organisation to support business strategy
- Contingency planning expertise/experience
- Ability to anticipate and avoid functional problems
- Ability to problem solve at the root cause level
- Ability to make and communicate hard decisions and courage to stay the course
- Ability to perform risk assessment
- Delegation skills
- Ability to select and assess sub-functional leaders based on function strategy
- Ability to empower
- Coaching direct reports and mentoring others
- Ability to drive cross-functional learning

People Development
- Team strength
- Succession
- Pipeline development
- Talent acquisition
- Personal learning leadership
- Coaching and mentoring
- Developing talent
- Cross-functional team exposure/rotation

- Full performance delivered by all direct reports and functional teamwork evident
- Ready now successor in place and leadership pipeline improves each year
- Right person in right job to deliver function results
- Coaching is a standard management routine (monthly performance discussions with direct reports with development dialogue two levels down on quarterly basis)
- Individual development plan implemented for all functional employees

- Team performs independent of Country Function Head
- Net supplier of talent

(Continued)

Function Manager (Continued)

Results	Full Performance	Exceptional Performance	Skills, Knowledge, and Experience
Leadership • Strategic vision; strategy • Change leadership • Performance/results culture • Functional capability • Personal business leadership • Enable functional leadership • Employee value proposition/ employer brand • Engagement satisfaction • Cross-functional teamwork	• Functional strategy developed demonstrated full understanding of market position and customer needs, was aligned to support corporate and business strategy and was communicated and accepted by the employees • Working environment created that encouraged constructive challenge and change • Poor performers addressed quickly at all levels in the function • Function's capability (including use of technology) enables business success • Personally connected to employees at all levels of the function • Lives corporate values, Code of Business Conduct and Code of Dealing for Employees • Import/export best practice • Engagement plan is in place and results improve year by year	• Function strategy copied by peers and competitors • Function's capability is at leading edge • Inspirational leadership • Role model for living corporate values and directives • Engagement results improved each year and meet or exceed service provider's database norms	• Ability to translate business strategy into function's • Ability to lead and manage change • Setting standards for function's performance • Confident in a leadership role • High integrity • Respectful of others, accepting/ adapting to local culture • Articulate communicator and effective listener at all layers • Cross-functional team building

Relationships
- Key customer/supplier relationships
- Relationships at all levels of the function
- Peer/corporate relationships
- Business/trade/industry groups/associations
- Union/work council relationships
- Educational institutions
- Community relations
- Public authorities relationships
- Opinion leaders and other important stakeholders

- Customer/supplier interface includes joint long-term functional planning
- Strong working relationships at all levels in the function enabled rapid communication
- Strong working relationships with each business team member and corporate assured mutual support
- Public authorities and other stakeholder relationships enabled effective management and co-operation

- Working relationships within the function strongest in the business
- Relationships with other functions created real teamwork
- Sought out by peers for coaching and strategic thinking

- Appreciate relationships for their own sake
- Ability to understand what drives people in other functions
- Knowledge of the contributions of all functions
- Well read in current events
- Understands the greater good
- Networking and lobbying skills

Growth and Innovation
- New markets
- New products
- New categories/channels
- New customers
- New applications/ processes
- New methods
- New ideas
- Corporate initiatives

- Function shows a stream of innovations and each direct report implemented at least one innovation
- Function processes continually improved, exploited growth opportunities and/or lowered cost and brought better results
- Corporate initiatives implementation (EATB, SAP etc.)
- Proactive functional best practices embedded and improved function's results and ineffective functional practices eliminated

- Breakthrough results achieved through industry leading practices
- New ideas acquired from studying parallel industries were applied

- Intellectual curiosity
- Open-minded and tolerant of difference
- Willingness to experiment and try new things
- Willingness to take risks and to learn from mistakes
- Experience in implementing innovation
- Process improvement skills
- Benchmarking of best practices

Social Responsibility (SR)
- Social responsibility awareness/behavior
- Consumer education
- Employer reputation
- Quality
- Safety and health
- Environment

- SR strategy and programs fully implemented in compliance with Guidelines on Environment, Marketplace, Community and Workplace
- Visible community leadership enhanced company's image
- Quality consistently at or above standards and met at optimal cost
- Ensured safety and health management systems and procedures are in place and followed

- Opportunities for partnering with community/government actively leveraged
- Social Responsibility Programs copied by peers and other competitors
- Quality improved significantly year after year

- Ability to see the social implications of function decisions
- Balanced judgment of impact and cost
- Ability to implement quality and safety and health management systems

Manager of Managers

Shift in Work Values

- From results through individuals to results through managers
- From individual productivity to management productivity
- From cross-team collaboration to subfunctional integration
- From work planning and performance management to operational planning
- From valuing work to valuing management
- From cross-boundary influence to effective functional team membership

Results	Full Performance	Exceptional Performance	Skills, Knowledge, and Experience
Business/Financial Results • Profit • Sales, volume • Cost control • Delivery of budget • Competitive analysis • Customer Satisfaction Index • Pricing	• All mission critical goals/KBIs met • Customer satisfaction improves year after year • Budgeted revenue, volume, cost, and programs delivered at optional cost • Customer engagement process enabled revenue growth • Pricing decisions reflect competitive reality	• Results enabled function to exceed plan • All mission critical goals/KBIs exceeded • Targets raised during business cycle met	• Understanding of financial impact of decisions • Ability to think tactically and strategically • Able to think in terms of functional sustainability rather than short-term wins • Must know how to read and interpret market data and competitive response • Cross-boundary thinking
People Development • Developing First-Line Mgrs • Team strength • Succession • Talent acquisition • Personal learning of leadership • Coaching and mentoring mgrs	• Full performance delivered by all First-Line Managers • Ready now successor in place and leadership pipeline improves each year • Right person in right job to deliver results • Individual development plan implemented for all employees • First-Line Managers taught to develop their people as part of day-to-day job	• Net supplier of management talent • First-Line Managers from other functions asked for coaching	• Ability to select and assess First-Line Managers • Ability to empower managers • Coaching direct reports and mentoring others • Ability to lead team learning events

Management			
Functional strategy execution	Function strategy executed at optimal cost	Project management practices copied by peers	Three to five years of managerial experience
Operational excellence	Right organisation, processes and systems in place to deliver sub-function results	Planning maximized overall synergies	Operational planning expertise/ experience
Project management	Infrastructure effectiveness enabled function's success while maintaining processes and systems	Resource management improved overall business results	Ability to anticipate and avoid operational problems
Operational planning	Business performance management system and tools for cross-functional boundary management fully utilised and outcomes measured with KBIs		Ability to problem solve at the root cause level
Strategic problem solving	Manpower and other resources trade-off decisions assured all plans were met		Ability to make and communicate hard decisions and courage to stay the course
Productivity	Projects completed on time and delivered real value to the business		Ability to manage managers
Compliance (EU, SOX etc.)			

Leadership			
Longer-term thinking	Function strategy understood and accepted by all sub-function members	Role model for living corporate values and directives	Ability to translate function strategy into sub-function's plan
Change leadership	Work environment created that encouraged constructive challenge and change	Strategy communication and engagement methods copied by peers	Ability to lead and manage change
Performance/results culture	Poor performers addressed quickly at all levels	Team effectiveness is greater than peers	Setting standards for management performance
Sub-functional capability	Sub-function's capability (including use of technology) enables success		Confident in a leadership role
Employee value proposition/ employer brand	Personally connected to employees at all levels of the function		Respectful of others, accepting/ adapting to local culture
Engagement satisfaction	Lives corporate values, Code of Business Conduct and Code of Dealing for Employees		Articulate communicator and effective listener at all layers
Cross-functional teamwork			Cross-functional team building

Relationships			
Key customer/supplier relationships	Customer/supplier interface includes win/win solutions	Working relationships within the function enabled functional synergy	Build relationships to improve results
Relationships at all levels of the function	Strong working relationships at all levels in the function enabled rapid communication	Relationships with peers in other functions created real teamwork	Ability to understand what drives peers in other functions
Cross-functional relationships	Strong working relationships with boss assured mutual support	Sought out by peers for coaching and problem solving	Knowledge of the contributions of all functions
Business/trade/industry groups/ associations	Mentoring relationship established with high performing individual contributors		Well read in current events
Union/work council relationships	Cross-functional relationships improved business results		Understands the greater good
Community relations			Ability to develop win/win solutions
Opinion leaders and other important stakeholders			

(Continued)

Manager of Managers (Continued)

Results	Full Performance	Exceptional Performance	Skills, Knowledge, and Experience
Growth and Innovation • New markets • New products • New categories/channels • New customers • New applications/ processes • New methods • New ideas	• Personally implemented at least one innovation • Processes continually improved, exploited growth opportunities and/or lowered cost and brought better results • Functional best practices embedded and improved results and ineffective practices eliminated • New programs/processes identified, sold and implemented	• New ideas acquired from studying parallel industries • Processes and programs widely used by other functions	• Learn from mistakes • Intellectual curiosity • Open-minded and tolerant of difference • Willingness to experiment and try new methods • Experience in implementing innovation without disruption • Process improvement skills
Social Responsibility (SR) • Policy dissemination • Social responsibility awareness/behavior • Consumer education • Employer reputation • Quality • Safety and health • Environment	• Ensured safety and health management systems and procedures are in place and followed by managers • Corporate SR strategy and programs fully understood and implemented in compliance with company Citizenship Guidelines on Environment, Marketplace, Community and Workplace • Quality consistently at or above standards and met at optimal cost	• Quality improved significantly year after year • Opportunities for partnering with community actively leveraged • Social Responsibility Programs copied by peers and other functions	• Ability to disseminate and enforce safety and environment policy • Balanced judgment of impact and cost of programs • Ability to implement quality, safety and health improvements

Manager of Others

Shift in Work Values

- From results through personal effort and cooperation to results through others
- From personal productivity to team productivity and individual productivity
- From working as a member of a team to building an effective and successful team
- From planning own work to work planning for team and performance management
- From valuing professional standards to valuing managerial work
- From developing high-quality individual work skills to developing managerial skills

Results	Full Performance	Exceptional Performance	Skills, Knowledge, and Experience
Professional/Technical/ Operational • KBIs delivery • Sales/volume/cost • Budget and expense management • Customer Satisfaction • Customer/vendor influence and decisions • Information analysis, sharing and reports • Project delivery	• Delivered product, service, advice to specification within budget and on time through team • All mission critical goals/KBIs met • Projects met all targets and helped deliver function strategy* • Customer Satisfaction surveys were analyzed and related action plans were developed • Management of customer (external/internal) engagement process enabled achievement of objectives • Advanced information on professional/ technical/ operational opportunities and changes shared appropriately • Right vendor delivered right services at right time for the right price* • Requested reports delivered accurately and on time	• All mission critical goals/ KBIs exceeded • New (additional) results achieved within budget • Extra value through customer and vendor partnerships	• General business practices • Ability to see the "big picture" • Ability to read and interpret market data and competitive response • Drive for results • Understanding of cost/revenue impact of decisions
People Development • Team strength • Team development • Coaching and feedback • Successor Development • Recruiting • Employee Training	• All team members have and use required technical competence • Coaching and feedback were part of day-to-day job and there were no surprises in the performance evaluation • All employees had a current development plan and were actively pursuing it • Identified successor's development plan was implemented • Right person in right job to deliver results • New hires have potential for bigger jobs	• Team members sought by other departments/ functions • Exceptional performers wanted to work on his/her team • Sought out as coach by other areas	• Identification and selection of talent • Coaching skills • Ability to create a learning environment • Teaching company's culture requirements • Feedback skills

(Continued)

Manager of Others (Continued)

Results	Full Performance	Exceptional Performance	Skills, Knowledge, and Experience
Management • Priorities • Work Plans • Execution and process management • Problem solving • Productivity • Compliance (EU, SOX, Audit, local tax and labor legislation, etc) • Project management	• Priorities for self and team established based on department/function objectives • All employees had clear direction, accountability, agreed upon current and measurable objectives • Control system ensured timely results and no surprises • Self & team in full compliance with internal policies, processes, standards and local legislation • Productivity increases each year; Self and team consistently reduced all non-value-adding work and waste	• Management practices copied by peers • Decision making, problem solving and compliance set the standards for peers' teams • Each individual and team in total met all goals	• Sub-function experience & expertise • Organizational and time management skills • Ability to anticipate and avoid problems • Ability to think logically • Ability to make quality decisions • Delegation skills • Full knowledge of function strategy • Project management skills • Knowledge and interpretation of policies, processes, procedures and systems • Sound judgment
Leadership • Translation of Group/ Country/Function strategic guidelines into local/departmental purpose and direction • Change leadership • Performance management • Employee retention • Motivation/recognition	• Group/Country/Function strategic guidelines were translated into local/departmental goals and direction* • Need for change was clearly communicated and accepted by the team • Regular recognition of employees produced increased performance • Poor performance addressed quickly • Lives corporate values and Code of Business Conduct (and Code of Dealing for Employees where applicable)	• Considered a role model for leading high performing and diverse front-line teams • Team effectiveness was greater than peers • Role model for living corporate values and directives at this layer	• Ability to interpret function strategy and culture* • Ability to implement change* • Ability to set clear standards for performance • High integrity • Ability to adapt leadership style appropriately • Ability to identify motivators key to individual performance • Conflict resolution

Relationships			
• Customers/vendors/suppliers • Functional stakeholders (peers, manager, functional community) • Opinion leaders and other important stakeholders • Cross-functional teamwork	• Customers/suppliers/vendors interface included win-win solutions • Open communication with peers and manager(s) assured "no surprises" • Trust and confidence developed with internal stakeholders • Cooperation with other functions ensured improved team's results	• Function relationships enabled country's/BU's/Group's unique needs to be met • Plans and goals reflected multi-unit thinking	• Ability to build relationships that enable results • Ability to communicate effectively • Country/BU business knowledge/awareness • Ability to read the situation and understand priorities • Knowledge of local needs and practices • Teamwork skills and mindset • Ability to develop win/win solutions
Growth & Innovation			
• New technical/operational/professional initiatives • New ideas • Technical/functional innovation • Systems, processes and standards improvement	• Track record of improvements driven by curiosity and application of new knowledge and ideas* • Relevant processes/programs continuously improved • Business initiatives were implemented successfully	• Team targets were exceeded through finding new ways of using function process/program improvements and new ideas • Continuous improvement was a "way of life" in the team	• Willingness to experiment and try new ideas • Process improvement skills • Product and industry knowledge • Benchmarking of best practices within own function
Social Responsibility			
• Policy understanding • Health, Safety & Environment • Employer reputation	• SR strategy and program fully understood and implemented as appropriate by the team • Health, safety & environment management systems and procedures in place and followed • Workplace conditions (physical) supported productivity, health and safety • Ensured that the company's local events enhanced the company's image* • Lives company Citizenship	• Opportunities for partnering with the community actively leveraged (e.g. speeches to educational institutions) • CSR programs copied by peers • Role model for company Citizenship in the Country	• Ability to disseminate and enforce health, safety & environment policy • Full knowledge of company's policies

*Indicates key new requirement for Manager of Others.

Self-Manager

Work Values
- Results through personal effort and often by cooperating with other teams
- Personal productivity
- Working as a member of a team
- Planning own work for personal success
- Valuing company and professional standards, adopting company's values and culture
- High-quality individual work and skills

Results	Full Performance	Exceptional Performance	Skills, Knowledge, and Experience
Professional/Technical/ Operational • Delivery of role's results • Customer service • Information sharing • Reports • Support in projects • KBI delivery	• Delivered work (products, analysis, support, services) and information on time and according to specifications • All mission critical goals/KBIs met • Customers were served according to the company's standards • Requested reports delivered accurately and on time	• Targets, due dates and quality standards regularly exceeded • All mission critical goals/ KBIs exceeded • New (additional) results achieved • Quality of work was model for peers	• Drive to learn fast and work independently • Basic financial understanding • Customer service mindset • Knowledge of functional needs • Ability to see the big picture
People Development • Self-development • Capability building in own area of work • Knowledge sharing and development	• Sharing/transferring of knowledge and information strengthened capability in the peer team • Demonstrated active learning through openness to feedback and application of professional/ technical/operational competence	• Peers sought to work with him/her in order to learn • Personal growth set standard for the team	• Openness to feedback • Self-assessment/awareness • Acquiring and applying new knowledge
Management • Work plans and priorities • Organization, check and control • Implementation of standards and specifications • Problem handling/solving • Productivity • Project management	• Work plans/project plans and priorities were based on departmental objectives • Checking and control routines ensured timely results and no surprises • Thorough implementation of the company's standards and specifications ensured no mistakes • Obstacles were handled and overcome in a timely manner • Productivity was increased due to optimal organization of work	• Time and work management improved departmental results • Problem handling/solving and implementation of company's standards and specifications set the norm for peers	• Attention to detail • Analytical skills • Ability to prioritize and plan • Ability to provide solutions to problems • Ability to perform repetitive duties according to standards

Leadership
- Values/ethics
- Teamwork/team play

- Contributed to positive teamwork environment consistently
- Personal behavior meets company's values/ethics requirements
- Went the extra mile with customers/peers

- Role model for living corporate values and directives
- Thought leader among peers

- Integrity
- Communication and effective listening skills
- Negotiation skills

Relationships
- Customers/vendors
- Functional stakeholders (peers, manager, functional community)
- Cross-functional teamwork

- Customer/vendor interactions facilitated achievement of department's objectives
- Cooperation with colleagues within own and with other functions ensured improved results
- Open communication in all directions assured "no surprises"

- Model for effective working relationships with peers in/outside function
- Plans and goals reflect multi-functional thinking

- Relationship building for supporting individual performance
- Team player
- Knowledge of goals and needs of other functions
- Knowledge of company's needs and practices in own function

Growth and Innovation
- New ideas
- Technical/functional innovation
- Service improvement
- Process improvement
- Internal/external benchmarking/best practices

- Track record of improvements driven by curiosity and application of new knowledge and ideas
- One innovation produced and considered for implementation each year
- Methods continuously improved
- Work routines adapted to fully support corporate initiatives, systems utilization and internal best practices

- Personal targets were exceeded through finding new ways of using function process/program improvements and new ideas
- New methods led to substantial productivity improvement in the team

- Intellectual curiosity
- Willingness to express and experiment new ideas
- Ability to learn from mistakes
- Information gathering

Social Responsibility (SR)
- Policy implementation
- Health, Safety & Environment
- Employer reputation

- SR strategy and program fully understood and followed
- Health, safety and environment management systems and procedures followed
- Reduced company's environmental impact (energy savings, paperless office etc.)
- Lives enterprise values

- Role model for enterprise citizenship
- Opportunities for partnering with community actively leveraged (as assigned)

- Full knowledge of enterprise's policies
- Understanding of environmental impact of own and others' work

Tool 2

Interview Questions

Questions and Probes	Listen for . . .
1A. Tell me about the scope of your job, e.g., number of people you manage, size of your budget, where does it fit in the value chain, etc. **Probe:** Where would you like more clarity?	• Completeness • Degree of complexity • Doing vs. managing for results • Level of enthusiasm
1B. Think broadly about expected results over the last two or three years. What are the key results expected from your position? *Probes:* *Consider other aspects of your work such as externals or softer areas (like people).* *You've given me a short list; consider all the ways you are measured.* **Note:** *Allow a little time for them to think.*	• Results by performance category: Financial/Operational, Management, Customer, Relationships, Leadership, Social Responsibility • Nouns, not verbs, e.g., plans not planning • Clarity of understanding of the job • Results focus vs. activity
2. What are the most important tasks you performed? **Probes:** *What do you actually do to achieve the results?* *I didn't hear any tasks associated with result XX—tell me what tasks are required.* *What are your tasks associated with risk management?*	• Verbs, no adverbs • Connection to the results, e.g., sales results require sales planning, sales calls, service visits

3A. Please give me some examples of important decisions you make.

Probes: Especially *what do you decide on their own?*

If none or small list of decisions is given probe: What recommendations do you make to your boss or others above you?

- Reasonable fit with required results
- Clarity of their authority
- Decisions vs. recommendations

3B. Any situations where you think you should have more authority?

Probe: Specifically, what must be decided by you in this job to be successful? Why is that authority needed?

- Connection to results
- Specificity of response vs. non-actionable idea
- Degree of thoughtfulness

4. What obstacles must be overcome to achieve your expected results?

Probes: Resources, politics, competition, management, skills, etc.

What are consequences or rewards for risk taking?

- Specificity of obstacles
- Breadth of the response, i.e., considers more than one kind of obstacle
- Relevance to results
- Internal vs. external

5. Describe for me how your time is spent, e.g., what percentage of the total is spent on each activity or result?

Probe: *For "meetings"—What is the purpose? Who called the meeting?*

For "customers"—what was the purpose of the interaction?

For "with my people"—doing what exactly?

- All tasks accounted for
- Enough specificity to discern what results category is being addressed
- Add up to 100%

Questions and Probes	Listen for . . .
6. What knowledge, skills, experience are required for success in the job? 16 A. Knowledge—technical, legal, customer-based, professional 16B. Skills—leading, managing, selling 16C. Experience—jobs, projects, geography, business type, line/staff **Probe:** How do these help overcome the obstacles? Help decision making?	• Consistency with results, tasks, obstacles • Thorough picture • Doing vs. leading • Technical vs. managerial
7. What has contributed the most to your preparation for this job? Was there a particularly important assignment, learning experience or mentor? **Probe:** *Why was this helpful?*	• Relevance to achieving results vs. relevance for getting selected for the job • Knowledge/Skill/Experience gained
8. What additional preparation would have been helpful? **Probe:** *It could be for making a particular decision or for executing a task.*	• Knowledge/Skill/Experience needed • Criticality of the issues in achieving results
9. Do you see any major changes in your position over the next 3 – 5 years? **Probe:** *How will [company name]'s strategy impact this job?*	• What results must change and why, what skills are needed • Driven by strategy change vs. expense reduction • Tailoring the job to the person

10. What additional development do you feel is needed to assure success in handling these changes?

- Job vs. project vs. training vs. coaching
- Knowledge/Skill vs. personal traits

11. Is cross-functional training (operations, finance, marketing, regulatory, corporate staff, etc.) necessary to do your job?

  Probe: What other functional experience would help achieve which results(s)?

- Connection to results
- Thoughtful answers
- **Not** knee-jerk reaction

12. Should cross-business training be encouraged?

  Probe: *Which businesses? What benefit would be obtained?*

- Connection to results
- Connection to Knowledge/Skills/Experience

13. Let's look at some key relationships that may impact your work.

13A. Describe your working relationships with your peers including peers in all Divisions/Businesses.

- Support vs. conflict
- Flow of information

13B. Describe your working relationships with your boss.

  Probe: What would you like to get from your boss that you aren't getting?

- Trust
- Guidance and coaching
- Mutual respect
- Unfulfilled needs

Acknowledgments

M any people helped me with this book in many different ways. While I can't possibly acknowledge individually everyone who contributed to my learning, special contributions were made by the following people.

Eric Drotter provided meaningful insights and heartfelt critiques that helped me get on the right path at the beginning and stay on it through to the end.

Bruce Wexler was invaluable in his editorial support, challenging both content and style while making the story flow more naturally.

Peter Burrow expanded my knowledge base on neuroscience and was a thoughtful collaborator in addressing the layer transition model.

Ram Charan encouraged and prodded me to write another book, just as he had done with *The Leadership Pipeline*.

My network of practitioners continuously engages me with application questions and opportunities while building performance pipelines themselves. Tom Flanagan, Barry Venter, Terry Gilliam, Peter Ivanoff, David Burrell, Greg Waldron, and Craig Mudge have been instrumental in advancing this work.

The Pipeline Users' Group has been a source of energy and useful feedback for me and for each other. Their willingness to share and debate has been of great learning value. The long-term members include Matt McGuire from Cancer Treatment Centers of America, Abby Curnow-Chavez from Newmont Mining, Zelia Soares from Murray & Roberts, David Daines and Denice Allen from Nu Skin, Sarah Robinson from Coca-Cola Hellenic, Kjetil Kristiansen from Aker Solutions, Joanne Best from QR National, and Samantha Wasserman.

As always, companies that invite me in to work on their challenges and opportunities provide the biggest impetus for learning. There isn't any substitute for getting into the details of how businesses and enterprises work at every level, and of what it takes to adapt to changing market conditions and evolving business strategy requirements. Without these experiences there wouldn't be a book. The learning continues with each new challenge.

Finally, Barbara Kostka worked tirelessly for days, nights, and weekends to get the manuscript into a presentable package.

The Author

STEPHEN DROTTER is chief executive of Drotter Human Resources, an executive succession planning, leadership performance, and organization design company serving a large global customer base. He has completed over forty enterprise-level CEO succession plans for corporations such as Citigroup, Goodyear, Marriott, Coca-Cola Hellenic, Ingersoll-Rand, Newmont Mining, DeBeers, and Cancer Treatment Centers of America. In-depth assessments of over 1,400 senior executives and the designing of forty major corporate organization structures have generated much of the information for this book. Steve has worked with over one hundred major corporations for more than one week. He has over forty-five years' experience in organization and management.

As an organization and management practitioner at GE, Steve was one of the early designers and implementers of GE's succession planning system. As Head of Human Resources, first at INA (now called Cigna) and then at Chase Manhattan, he focused on executive succession, leadership performance and development, and organization design. He was a member of the Policy Committee at both companies.

Steve is coauthor of *The Leadership Pipeline: How to Build the Leadership-Powered Company* (Jossey-Bass, 2000, 2011) and *The Succession Planning Handbook for the Chief Executive* (Mahler Press, 1985). He holds a degree in economics from Amherst College and is a graduate of GE's Human Resources Program.

Steve can be reached at SJDrotter@aol.com.

Index

Business level, additional results
expected at the, 195
Business Managers: in an actual
Performance Pipeline, *264–265*;
addressing issues with, example of,
CEOs role in, 48–49; balanced
engagement by, need for, 123;
broadening the range of results for,
example of, 26; building succession
for, 71; and capital allocation, 74;
coaching, 77–78, 90; competing
with, 90; critical results for,
94–105; defacto, 94; defining the
role of, 93, 94; development of,
77–78; enabling better decision
making by, 74; expected results for,
94–109, *264–265*; failure rate of,
93; focus of, in the Performance
Pipeline, *14*; former, hanging on
to the role, issue of, 79; founders
as, 130; inappropriate results for,
110–111; interviewing, 29;
involvement of Group Managers
in the strategy produced by,
76–77, 90; issues with developing,
case involving, 17; managers
reporting to, 113, 114; and
narrowly focused Function
Managers, example of, 115, 116;
natural progression of work values
for, examples of, *38, 39*; passage of,
in the Leadership Pipeline model,
13; performance standards for,
developing, example of, 105–109;
portfolio strategy helping, 76; and
tailored pipelines, 248; technical
guidance provided to, 113; whole
job results for, 105–109. *See also*
Profit layer
Business results: for Business
Managers, 95–101, *106, 264*;
driver of, Technical Performance
Pipeline as a, 193; for Enterprise
Managers, 51, 52–57; for Function
Managers, 120–121, 122, 124, *125*,
127, 266; for Group Managers, 75,

87, *262*; having evidence of,
example of, 254; for Managers of
Managers, *270*; for Managers of
Others, 166, 168; for Self-
Managers, 188
Business rhythm, steady, delivering a,
102–103
Business strategy: changing, keeping
up with, 184; Enterprise Managers
responsible for the, 58; executing
a, critical ingredients for, 95;
involvement level of Group
Managers in the, 76–77, 90; in the
Performance Pipeline, 11

C

Capital allocation, 73–74
Caring, balanced, 153–154, 158
Change: context, commitment to,
203–204, 223; industry, leading,
196; needed, using transitions for,
240–241; in the performance
management process, 42;
resistance to, 190, 203–204, 223,
258; ripple effect of, 25; slower,
124; symbiotic relationship
between results and, 211. *See also*
Innovation
Chief Executive Officer (CEO),
enterprise-wide. *See* Enterprise
Managers/CEOs
Chief Financial Officer (CFO): and
capital allocation, 74; as a CEO
succession candidate, 91; in
customer companies, Self-
Managers doing business with, 39;
founders/CEOs as the, 130; lack of
a, addressing, example of, 48, 49;
lacking in accountability for
enterprise results, example of, 72.
See also Function Managers
Chief Operating Officer. *See* Group
Managers
Citigroup, 12
Citizenship, good, 183–184
Clarity. *See* Role clarity

G